THE HOME FRONT
WORLD WAR II
1939 - 1945

by

Stanley Naylor

Dedicated to:
Marie Curie Cancer Care
and
Macmillan Cancer Relief

Cover photographs:

Top: Boston Stump - the largest Parish Church in Great Britain and used for navigation by air crews in World War II.

Middle: Illustration of the famous Lancaster Bomber.

Bottom: AFS crew ready for action, Isle of Dogs, East London 1939/40.
Bottom picture produced by kind permission of Island History Trust.

THE HOME FRONT
WORLD WAR II
1939 - 1945

by

Stanley Naylor

Written, compiled and first published in Great Britain in the year 2001 by Stanley Naylor.

Copyright © Stanley Naylor 2001.

British Library Cataloguing in Publication Data.

ISBN 0-9527846-5-3

All rights reserved. No part of this publication may be reproduced, stored in a retrieval system or transmitted in any form or by any means, electronic, mechanical, photocopying, recorded or otherwise, without prior permission in writing from the publisher. The information contained herein is from the author's own knowledge and sources believed to be reliable, but accuracy cannot be guaranteed.

Printed by:
Guardian Press (Boston) Ltd.
Nelson Way
Boston
Lincolnshire, PE21 8TS
United Kingdom

CONTENTS

Acknowledgements 5-7
Introduction 8-9
Speech by King George VI 10-11
Poem: Our Finest Hour - unknown author 12
The Home Front World War II 1939 - 1945 by Stanley Naylor . 13-23
The Home Front 1939 - 1945 by Len Cuttler 24-33
Recollections of the Second World War Period in Kirton,
   Boston, Lincolnshire by Colin Cumberworth 34-45
Wartime Memories 1939 to 1945 by Jack Cumberworth 46-47
A Wartime Childhood in Lincoln by Maureen Street 48-51
Poem: Were You At Dunkirk? by Victor Cavendish 52
The Home Guard On Parade 53-55
Home Guard Certificate - Horace Chambers 56
The British Resistance Organisation 1940 to 1944 57-64
Here's the reason for a red face - Fred Fossitt 65
The Royal Observer Corps 66-67
The Island at War - Eve Hostettler 68-73
Women's Institute 74-76
Poem: A Knitting Lyric - unknown author 77
The Royal Air Force 78-81
Poem: Stand Those Three Towers by Victor Cavendish 82-83
A Brief History of Air Sea Rescue Operations by G R Chaters . 84-100
Weekend Leave 101-105
Poem: A Prayer For You by John R Walsh 106
The United States Army Air Force 107-114
Beaufighter Versus Dornier by David Stubley 115-118

The Mail Train by Jim Jackson 119-120
No. 4 RAF Hospital Rauceby by Gwyneth Stratton 121-123
Poem: High Flight 124
The Lancaster Memorial - Sibsey Northlands 125-129
Poem: Lancaster Memorial - Sibsey Northlands 130
The Lancaster Memorial - Ulceby Cross 131-132
Poem: Lethal Lady by John R Walsh 133
A Brief History of the Second World War by Margaret Allen . 134-136
Wartime Recipes 137-147
Photographs 148-170
Advertisements 171-203
List of Abbreviations 204-206
Two maps from 1944 207-208
Highly recommended books 209-210
Advertisement for a previous book by the same author 211
A list of relevant museums 212-214

ACKNOWLEDGEMENTS

Many of the stories produced in this book have been given to me and I therefore wish to express my thanks and appreciation to each of the authors and to other sources from which I have gathered information. Without your generous contribution of providing material, photographs and documents, the completion of this book would not have been possible. It has been a privilege talking to many of you and share your experiences. I have been enriched and often humbled, by the determination to carry on despite the bombs, blackout and rationing, by those of you who lived through the war years.

Jessie and Eddie Welberry, Kirton Holme. Eddie related the story on the 'Secret Army' and loaned me a lot of information. Interviewed 2001. Plus I gleaned some information from 'The Last Ditch' by David Lampe, published by Cassell of London 1968.

Mr Geoff Hadfield, Alford, for the information on the Royal Observer Corps and the Memorial at Ulceby Cross. Interviewed 2001.

Mr James P. Allen and Change Charity, Yeovil, for permission to reproduce 'A Brief History of the Second World War' and 'A Wartime Childhood in Lincoln' by Maureen Street, from the magazine 'Civilians at War'. Letter 2001.

David Stubley, Frampton, first gave me the story on 'Beaufighter versus Dornier' for my book 'Memories' in 1996 and kindly permitted me to reproduce it in this book. Telephone conversation 2001.

Jim Jackson, Boston, likewise gave me the story on 'The Mail Train' for my book 'Memories' in 1996 and kindly permitted me to reproduce it in this book. Letter 2001.

Mrs Gwyneth Stratten, North Rauceby, also gave me the story on 'No. 4 RAF Hospital Rauceby' for my book 'Memories' in 1996 and kindly permitted me to reproduce it in this book. Telephone conversation 2001.

Len Cuttler, Boston; Pete Usher, Woodhall Spa and Dave Russell,

Canada, for the local story on the 'Home Front' involving the Kirton District. Telephone conversation and letter 2001.

Mrs H. A. Hall, Kirton, for the information on the Women's Institute. Interviewed 2001.

Colin Cumberworth, Boston and Jack Cumberworth, Peterborough, for their memories and recollections of Kirton during the war years. Phone calls and letter 2001.

Graham Richard Chaters, Secretary Humber Branch Air Sea Rescue Marine Craft Sections Club, Grimsby, for the brief history of Air Sea Rescue operations around Lincolnshire during the war years. Telephone and letter 2001.

Thomas Henry and Nora Wilson, Stickney, for their eye witness account of the crashed Lancaster Bomber at Sibsey Northlands. Interviewed 2001.

John Edward Callaby, Bicker, for his account of the Lancaster Bomber that crashed at Sibsey Northlands. Interviewed 2001.

Eve Hostettler and Island History Trust for the reproduction of photographs and extracts from her book 'The Island At War'. Letters 2001.

Jim Fossitt - the story on the reason for his father's red face, as printed in the Boston Standard.

The British Library for the reproduction of advertisements, recipes and other material from film of the Boston Guardian newspapers published from 1939 to 1945 and held at the Boston Library.

David Sarson, curator of the 388th Bomb Group Collection, for information on USAAF plus story and photo of 'Glancey's Bag'. Visit June 2001.

Fred and Harold Panton, Lincolnshire Aviation Heritage Centre, East Kirkby, for information on the airfield and permission to take and use photographs. Visits and telephone call 2001.

Lillian Ream Collection, Wisbech, for the use of photographs. Visits in April/May 2001 and letter?

Allied Forces Military Museum, Stickford, Mr Houldershaw, for the searchlight photograph.

The ladies in both Boston and Kirton libraries, for their unstinting help in locating books and film.

Joan Dixon for the reproduction of her father's Home Guard certificate.

John Walsh my late poetic friend for the publishing rights of all his poems.

Victor Cavendish for permission to use his poems - 'Stand Those Three Towers' and 'Were You At Dunkirk?'

Military Airfields in the British Isles 1939 - 1945 by Steve Willis and Barry Hollis published by Enthusiasts Publications. Unfortunately I was unable to contact the publishers, but acknowledge using facts and figures extracted from the book relating to the RAF stations on which I served from 1941 to 1944.

The East Anglia Tourist Board for permission to use extracts from the Official Souvenir Guide of The USAAF Reunion 1992. Letter 28th August 2001.

Chris Williams for many hours freely spent proof reading.

Staff at Guardian Press for producing the book, in particular Mandy for her design skills.

Should I have inadvertently omitted to acknowledge any source of information contained in this book, then I offer my sincere apologies.

Stanley Naylor, 2001

INTRODUCTION

'The Home Front World War II 1939 to 1945' follows on from my previous book - Lincolnshire Country Life Beside the Wash 1920's to 1939, published in September 2000.

I suppose it could be said that it is a journey into the past, but I believe there is an awful lot of information known by ordinary people, the people who were in the thick of everyday activities, that needs to be written for posterity. Hoping of course, that future generations will never have to suffer the traumas of war that those of my generation suffered.

The original idea was to write about my local area, but it was then realised that 'The Home Front' involved everyone, man, woman and child in the British Isles, whether civilian or serving in HM Forces. I have therefore endeavoured to portray how each person fitted into the jigsaw and was a vital link in defending our shores from the Nazi regime.

It has been a learning process in researching the mere handful of stories contained within these pages, they are a cross section of the hundreds that I'm sure could be told!

However, many things have come to light, for example, I know more about the 'Secret Army' (The Resistance Organisation) that appeared to operate under the umbrella of the Home Guard. In fact their role was entirely different and would have been extremely risky had there been an invasion.

The Royal Observer Corps played a vital role in identifying aircraft from their strategic positions around the British Isles. They also took part in the 'D' Day operation in assisting as aircraft spotters on board troop ships.

Cities and towns suffered horrendous bombing, but none worse than the 76 consecutive nights - with a break of only one night - suffered by London that commenced on the 7th September 1940. Air raid shelters, sandbags, tin hats and gas masks were therefore a common sight and the comradeship between people of all walks of life was terrific.

The girls in the Land Army seemed to have been forgotten, but their work on the farms was a valuable contribution in providing essential food, not just for civilians, but also the troops. In fact growing food was an essential part in the defence of Great Britain. Some sixty per cent of our food was being imported at the outbreak of hostilities, so with forty-eight million mouths to feed, the plough became a weapon of war. Therefore the effort to produce more food and the slogan 'Dig for Victory', put a great strain on the farming community that was suffering from a shortage of labour. Hence the reason the Land Army Girls played such a vital role in this countryside industry.

Women's Institute, Women's Volunteer Service, Air Raid Wardens, Firemen, Police, Ambulance Crews, Doctors, Nurses, the Army guarding our shores, Bomber and Fighter air crews with their ground staff based on home stations pitted against the Luftwaffe and even the evacuees, were all linked together in the struggle of survival.

Rationing was essential and a copy of the cover of a ration book has been reproduced with some of the amounts allocated per person. Many wartime recipes using basic ingredients were introduced and a sample is included. With travel being restricted, local sporting activities were popular and even football pools existed, a copy of a rare football coupon can be seen later in the book. Prices in the adverts are astounding, rare photographs recall nostalgic memories and the poems have been chosen to fit in with the stories.

After the fall of France, signposts were dismantled, street names and even names on farm vehicles were obliterated in order to confuse an invading German Army. But see copies of German Maps I acquired when in France in 1944, the Germans would have had no problem finding their way around the United Kingdom.

Since the ending of World War II, the phases - 'Before the War', 'During the War' and After the War', are often used. The war therefore being a significant phase in peoples lives, recalling memories that are etched in their minds and cannot be erased.

Stanley Naylor, 2001

SPEECH BY KING GEORGE VI

Just after 11 o'clock on Sunday 3rd. September 1939, the British Prime Minister informed the nation that we were at war with Germany. That evening King George VI broadcast the following message to his people.

"In this grave hour, perhaps the most fateful in our history, I send to every household of my people, both at home and overseas, this message, spoken with the same depth of feeling for each one of you as if I were able to cross your threshold and speak to you myself.

For the second time in the lives of most of us we are at war. Over and over again we have tried to find a peaceful way out of the differences between ourselves and those who are now our enemies.

But it has been in vain. We have been forced into a conflict. For we are called with our allies to meet the challenge of a principle which, if it were to prevail, would be fatal to any civilised order in the world.

It is the principal which permits a State, in the selfish pursuit of power, to disregard it's treatment and its solemn pledges; which sanctions the use of force, or threat of force, against the sovereignty and independence of other States.

Such a principal, stripped of all disguise, is surely the mere primitive doctrine that might is right; and if this principle were established throughout the world, the freedom of our own country and of the whole British Commonwealth of Nations would be in danger.

But far more than this - the peoples of the world would be kept in the bondage of fear and all hopes of settled peace and of the security of justice and liberty among nations would be ended.

This is the ultimate issue which confronts us. For the sake of all that we ourselves hold dear and of the world's order and peace, it is unthinkable that we should refuse to meet the challenge.

It is to this high purpose that I now call my people at home and my peoples across the seas, who will make our cause their own. I ask them to stand calm and firm and united in this time of trial.

The task will be hard. There may be dark days ahead and war can no longer be confined to the battlefield. But we can only do the right as we see the right and reverently commit our cause to God.

If one and all we keep resolutely faithful to it, ready for whatever service or sacrifice it may demand, with God's help, we shall prevail."

"May He bless and keep us all."

"I have nothing to offer but blood, toil, tears and sweat, to wage war against monstrous tyranny, never surpassed in the dark, lamentable catalogue of human crime".

Winston Churchill on becoming Prime Minister, May 1940

OUR FINEST HOUR

This truly is our 'Finest Hour',
When we alone are left to bear
    The shining torch of free men's power
That lights the darkness of despair!

Remember Drake? He lived again
In every British man-o-war!
    In ev'ry 8 gun fighter 'plane,
In ev'ry army, ev'ry corps.

That comes to us across the sea;
In fact, in ev'ry British heart
    That beats wherever men are free
And wish, each one, to play a part.

In this magnificent crusade
This war of Evil versus Good
    This clash that brings a cavalcade
Of international brotherhood.

In one long never-ending stream
From ev'ry corner of the earth
    Resolved to smash a tyrant's dream
And help to give a New World birth!

P.R.
Boston Guardian, September 1940
By permission of the British Library

THE HOME FRONT
WORLD WAR II - 1939 to 1945
by
Stanley Naylor

I was fortunate to have been born in the flat Fenland's of Lincolnshire, where fresh air was the norm and Mother Nature taught us the facts of life! As children we roamed the meadows, lanes and the marsh in the North/West corner of the Wash at our leisure, without fear of being molested or abducted. The close knit community in which we lived, kept a watchful eye on all its children without being intrusive that gave us the freedom we enjoyed. There were unwritten rules, of course, the law of the land was obeyed and any wrongdoing was severely reprimanded by teachers at school and at home by loving parents who tried to keep us on the straight and narrow! School attendance was from 9.00am to 3.30pm Monday to Friday and very few played truant. Sunday School was at the Chapel for one hour, 11.00am to midday.

To my knowledge, there was no problem in getting a job on leaving school at the age of fourteen, farming being the obvious choice. Agriculture demanded a large labour force throughout the spring, summer and autumn months to harvest all the crops. Late potatoes for example, required a gang of ten/twelve people - mainly women - picking behind a spinner drawn by three horses and driven by one man. Two men emptied laden mollies into a moving horse drawn cart and another man had the task of storing the tubers in a grave, or clamp. Then during the winter months the potatoes would be sorted, bagged and transported to various markets in the UK.

Life therefore, revolved around the seasons on the farm, then 1939 dawned, a good summer prevailed with the usual large crowd of people attending the annual 'mud lark' down Kirton Marsh on August Bank Holiday Monday and the harvest was safely gathered in! However, things had already begun to change in this close knit community and tranquil countryside that would never be the same again. The Government had issued gas masks and Air Raid Precautions were in place. Then late on Friday afternoon on the 1st September 1939 a contingent of soldiers from the Essex Regiment, London district, arrived complete with searchlight and generator. Tents were pitched in a three-cornered grass field beside the Roman Bank on the Kirton Marsh Road and the new residents became part of the Fenland community.

War had been talked about on the wireless and in the papers and, no doubt, in the pubs, the 'Boat & Gun' for example, but the Prime Minister had tried hard to get a peace agreement with Hitler that failed. Therefore at 11.00am on Sunday 3rd September 1939, the BBC informed British Radio listeners to stand-by for an announcement by the Prime Minister. A few minutes later the PM, the Rt. Hon. Neville Chamberlain, announced to the British people that Hitler had been requested to withdraw his troops from Poland. 'I have to tell you now', he said, 'that no such undertaking has been received and that consequently this country is at war with Germany'. France joined later that day, as also did two British Dominions, Australia and New Zealand.

This was the start of the Second World War, in which I don't suppose we really wanted to get involved, the 1914 - 1918 conflict was still remembered by the older generation, but we had no choice, we were committed. Whereas the First World War did not come to Britain, this War was going to affect the lives in one way or another of everyone on this small island. Rationing became inevitable because of the deadly activities of German submarines disrupting supplies from overseas, long range bombers and 'doodle bugs' caused destruction to towns and cities and, the most devastating of all, the loss of loved ones had a traumatic effect on our daily lives.

Although in 1939/40 life did not seem to alter very much, we still worked 7.00am to 4.00pm, the normal working day on the farm and most evenings in the summer from 5.00pm to 8.00pm.

During the first eighteen months of the War, we still paid our weekly visit to Boston on a Saturday night, having the choice of four cinemas was a luxury. The New Theatre and Scala in the Market Place had been showing films for more years than I could remember and at the outbreak of the war was still very popular. At that time in comparison was the Regal Cinema in West Street, showing Shirley Temple in her first colour movie, 'The Little Princess'. In South Square was the magnificent

Odeon Cinema showing 'Wuthering Heights' starring Merle Oberon, Laurence Olivier and David Niven. Roller-skating was popular at a new rink at the Gliderdrome in Boston, but it was of no interest to me.

Farming did, of course, play its part in the war, every piece of available land was put under the plough. More than half of our food was being imported at the outbreak of war, so it was crucial that Great Britain became as near as possible to being self-sufficient in food production. Arable land increased almost three-fold and there was a problem with a shortage of male workers, hence the reason for the women taking on more jobs.

THE WOMEN'S LAND ARMY (WLA)

In the very early part of the war, thousands of girls (young women in fact) joined the WLA, most of them I believe to be volunteers, although they may not have had a personal choice because help was badly needed on farms with the 'Dig for Victory' campaign. More land was being put under the plough and men were leaving the farms and joining the Armed Forces. The WLA numbered some 80,000 and they came from all walks of life including secretaries, waitresses and shop assistants who were pitched into a country life with no mod cons, which many had been used to in the towns and cities from which they came. Their uniform became a familiar part of the farming fraternity consisting of brown felt hats, cotton blouses, green jerseys and brown breeches, the latter being a very good choice for working in all weathers on the farm.

Unfortunately I never had the privilege to work with any of them and only came in contact with them when on leave! I understand they brought a breath of fresh air to mundane work, even though the farming fraternity was of the opinion they were getting useless girls who would be an hindrance through not having the skills and the strength required to perform many of the strenuous tasks on the farms.

The girls found that rural life had many discomforts that were taken for granted by local residents. First of all, in many cases, because there was no running water, they had to get used to bathing in a tin tub and the privy would be outside in the yard that had a wooden seat over a vault. On many farms there was no electricity, although some did have their own portable generator. There would be no gas either, cooking would be done on an open coal fire, or if they were lucky there would be an Aga cooking range. They would then find that rats, mice and creepy-crawlies and perhaps an odd grass snake, were all part and partial of farming. Then there were the elements to contend with, animals have to be fed seven days a week come rain or shine and I know, for example, that pulling brussel sprouts on a cold frosty morning is no picnic, also pulling and knocking sugar beet after a heavy rain is horrendous!

In spite of all these things, the girls settled down and did a remarkable job that surprised many of their employers and the male workers, although some may not have admitted it, even admired their guts. They learned to work with horses, drive tractors, planted and weeded potatoes and when harvested carried bags that weighed no less than eight stone (112 lbs). I don't expect they attempted to carry eighteen stone of corn (252 lbs), but they did learn how to milk cows and then muck-out the cow shed and also the pig sty, the latter I can assure the reader expelled a much more pungent aroma.

Therefore these girls, who took a lot of pride in what they were doing, did a tremendous job in helping to feed the Nation. They were demobbed gradually after the war and finally the WLA era ended in 1951. As far as I am aware, their contribution to the war effort was never officially recognised. However, many of them found husbands and settled in the area in which they had been working.

FORESTRY AND MUNITIONS

My information on girls working in the woods and forests is sparse. About 1942 a Women's Timber Corps was established and the girls were known as Lumber Jills. Timber was in great demand for all sorts of things including pit props and poles. Therefore their job in felling trees to provide the timber for the war effort, was just as important as the work the WLA were doing on the farms.

Thousands of girls worked in munitions, again my information is sparse. However, my wife experienced three months in munitions at Burslem, Staffordshire, during one winter when work was slack on a local farm. Being an out-door girl, shift work did not suit her, or the constant working in a confined space under artificial lights. She was pleased when Spring arrived and her farmer employer found her work back at home.

Working in munitions and aircraft factories were occupations, like the WLA, were of vital importance where the girls did a tremendous job producing guns and ammunition that was needed by the Armed Forces. Many girls also worked in other occupations, including joining the Armed Forces that helped the war effort.

Therefore each and every girl did her bit no matter what occupation she was in on the Home Front, it all culminated in **Victory in Europe** and later **Victory over Japan**.

BLACKOUT

The Blackout commenced on 1st September 1939 and ended on 17th September 1944, when all hostilities had ceased. There was a problem at nights that first winter, and perhaps the following winters, with an increase in accidents and casualties and trying to abide by the rules that came under the umbrella of the ARP (Air Raid Precautions). Car headlamps had to be fitted with the regulation ARP masks that only permitted a glimmer of light and cycle lights had to be dimmed, as also did torches. Not a ray of light was permitted from windows of houses, the smallest chink brought an Air Raid Warden demanding the offending light be obliterated. Subsequently some of these unlucky ARW's, who were only doing their duty for the safety of the offending citizens in trying to preserve their lives, became hated figures, on a par, I suppose, as Traffic Wardens are in our society today!

People in the towns being used to streets lights, even though some of the streets were dimly lighted, found it difficult walking in the blackout. It was not so difficult in the country, we were used to finding our way around on dark nights, often aided by the moon. One thing was certain that is not so today, everyone, including the women folk of all ages, could freely walk anywhere without fear of being attacked and robbed.

Darkness only existed outside the house, although lighting in the homes were not very good consisting of paraffin lamps, both hanging from the ceiling and free standing and candles. Electricity and gas had not reached many outlying districts including Kirton Skeldyke. In the depth of winter it was dark going to work on the farm in the morning and dark by the time workers arrived home at night. The wireless helped to while away long dark evenings and popular programmes were 'ITMA' (It's That Man Again) starring Tommy Handley. 'The Brains Trust', Vera Lynn presenting 'Sincerely Yours', George Formby with his ukulele singing - 'When I'm Cleaning Windows'. Gracie Fields was affectionately known as 'Our Gracie' and 'Uncle Mac', in 'Children's Hour' was a favourite with children.

Various activities became popular including darts, card games, assembling jigsaw puzzles and many people turned to reading books. It was also an opportunity to make a snip-rug. This involved finding old clothes such as jackets and trousers and cutting them in strips five or six inches in length and one to one and a half inches wide. A clean hessian sack would be cut open and used to attach the strips of clothing, colours being clustered to form patterns. This rug, costing nothing in material, was very hard wearing and had pride of place in front of the fire. Knitting, of course, was the domain of the women, who could talk, listen to the wireless and click away with needles, producing some useful garments at very little cost.

Sick and Dividing Clubs were popular, there being no National Health Service, and I was a member of one at Kirton Skeldyke from 1936 to 1941. Where was their H.Q? At the local pub, of course, the 'Boat & Gun', which was very popular for a country hostelry. These Clubs provided a member with financial help when ill on production of a Doctor's certificate and a dividend was very useful at Christmas. Organising events such as a sports day and whist drives to raise funds was popular with local residents. Therefore these Clubs not only provided financial assistance in time of need, but also cheap and useful entertainment.

The dark nights during winter meant longer hours on duty for the soldiers manning the search light, but they still found time to visit their local watering hole, the 'Boat & Gun'. This was also a favourite with my father who enjoyed conversation with the soldiers on his usual Friday night visits. This resulted in some of the soldiers being invited in two's for Sunday tea at our house, father perhaps remembering being away from home during his horrendous war service 1914 to 1918. The soldiers also provided all the ingredients and receptacles for mother to make them huge meat and taty pies and bread puddings. Their loaves were long and square and, I must say, it was very tasty bread!

EVACUATION

An evacuee was a person sent away from a dangerous area and was a new word to appear in the English language in 1939/1940. School children, blind people, invalids and expectant mothers were moved out of London - and other cities and towns - to what was thought to be safe areas. I'm not so sure that the area around the Wash was all that safe. There were bombs dropped haphazardly from escaping German aircraft chased by RAF fighters and see copies later in the book of two maps of Lincolnshire that I acquired when in France in 1944. The county would not have been safe had any German troops been permitted to invade the territory around the Wash.

It was in early 1940 that my family moved from one cottage, namely the 'Tin Huts' a product of the First World War, to Bucklegate Cottage on the same farm. My father was wagoner on the middle farm of three owned by Mr Henry Tunnard. Our new abode was an old fashioned four bedroom brick house situated down a lane with grass growing in the centre that could only be called a farm track. Even so, it was the only access to Bucklegate Cottage and at least four more houses. We had no en-suite facilities, the only bath was a large tin tub that had to be filled and emptied with a bucket, with the water being heated in a copper. The privy (toilet) was a small brick building down the garden path with a wooden seat over a vault that had to be emptied once a year, or more often with a large family! It has already been mentioned that paraffin lamps and candles were the only means of lighting.

It must have been a shock therefore for Mrs Sparrey and her three sons, Stanley, Gerald and Michael, when they left the mod cons of their Highgate home in London and joined us in this Fenland area deprived of those facilities. Len Sparrey stayed in London to carry on his job as a chauffeur for a large firm, he was also a member of the ARP (Air Raid Precautions) service. Len paid a few visits to see his family, however he didn't like driving on our narrow roads with dykes on each side, he preferred the hustle and bustle of the crowded city. Stanley, the elder of the boys, recalls working on a local farm performing jobs that we country lads know only too well! One precarious job was standing on the platform of a threshing machine cutting bands as the sheaves of corn was placed in the arms of the man feeding them into the beaters. The string made the left hand very sore and if it was barley being threshed, which Stanley reminded me, the horns would get attached to both hands and clothing, very uncomfortable! Stanley also recalls picking potatoes (tates in farming jargon) that was a back-breaking job, which is now all completed by modern machinery.

However, in spite of the fact that the two families came from completely different backgrounds, we became firm friends, as no doubt did many evacuees and their country families. After hostilities ceased and life began the long haul of returning to normal, Highgate became our base for exploring the big city.

Children from the cities and towns arriving in the country for the first time were terrified of cows and sheep grazing peacefully in green meadows. Meek and mild rabbits frightened some of them and the wise old owl hooting in the night kept many of them awake. All these things we took for granted through our childhood and, of course, in this Fenland area, we were true 'Yellowbellies'.

FOOD RATIONING

With the threat of war eminent in Europe, it was as early as 1938 that

Britain prepared to organise a rationing system Coal was one of the first things to be rationed and by the end of 1939 ration books had been issued that enabled food rationing to be introduced in Great Britain in January 1940. The weekly ration per adult was not easy to get accustomed, here are some examples:

Butter 2 oz — Margarine 4 oz — Cooking Fat 4 oz — Cheese 2 oz - Sugar 8 oz — Ham and Bacon 4 oz - Eggs 1 shell egg a week - Meat - 1s. 6d. worth per week (approximately 7p in today's currency) Sweets - 12 oz per month.

Bread was never rationed, but speaking from experience, the so-called 'National Loaf' was not all that appetising. Dried milk and dried eggs appeared in the shops and I don't recall tinned goods being popular before 1939, but they became essential during the war years, even for country folk. Living in the country, of course, was an asset, most households had a large garden that produced a lot of vegetables, any short fall was purchased cheaply off the farm and in many cases were deemed part of the perks! 'Dig For Victory', was a familiar slogan, so allotments were popular, some of them being an acre in size, this being a manageable piece of land for a working man. A few chickens laid enough eggs for a family. A sty at the bottom of the garden housed a pig that not only devoured household waste, but also produced enough meat for a year for an average family. It was known for a large family to kill two pigs in a year, where else could meat be obtained so cheaply?

'Make do and mend' was a slogan born from necessity. I was taught to sew buttons on trousers and darn socks by my Grandfather in the early 1930's. It was not realised at that time how these two domestic jobs were to be useful a few years later when I joined the RAF Regiment.

Clothes were referred to as utility and non-utility and purchased on production of coupons. Ladies hats were in short supply so they adapted scarves that became a popular headdress. Tights were unheard of and stockings required coupons, rayon easily laddered, so the girls covered their legs with sun tan lotion. This was successful and very effective on a nice summers evening, but disastrous when it rained!

Footwear required coupons, but the 'make do and mend' spirit prevailed that kept cobblers busy nailing on new soles and heels that was much cheaper than buying new boots and shoes. The leather was thick, heavy and hardwearing, this proved to be all right on boots, but tended to make shoes clumsy.

I am informed that commodities not rationed were often in short supply. Washing powder such as Persil and Rinso were difficult to find so flakes of kitchen soap would be used. Washing was done by hand in a tub with the clothes being turned with a five-legged dolly peg. The next stage was the clothes were boiled in a copper then put through a wringer, or mangle, as it was often referred, to squeeze out as much water as possible. Finally they would be hung on a line beside a garden path to be dried by Mother Nature. All of this a far cry from automatic washing machines of today!

Petrol rationing did not affect many families, a few people had motor cycles but cars were few and far between. However, in November 1939 hauliers were protesting at an inadequate supply of fuel, mainly caused no doubt by the dreaded German Submarines intercepting tankers on their way from distant countries.

Cycles were the main form of transport and a cyclist in November 1939 was fined 5/- (25p) for showing too much light, the magistrate informed the offending person to be more careful in the future. Then in November 1940, a number of cyclists were summoned for not showing a rear light, not just at night, but also on the way to work in a morning. Their fines are not known, but I am informed the maximum penalty was £100 or three months in prison.

In January 1941 the Ministry of Home Security reminded torch users that torches were required at all times to have the aperture reduced to a diameter of one inch and the light dimmed by the insertion of one thickness of newspaper or the equivalent. There was no difference in this respect between the 'Alert' and other periods.

British restaurants were found in all parts of the country. The first one to open in the rural district of Boston was at the Black Bull in Kirton in November/December 1941. The restaurant was very popular with school children and had a considerable adult patronage, proving to be a model for future ventures in the district. The Women's Volunteer Service (WVS) manned the restaurants, hostels, nurseries, rest centres and, no doubt, took on many other jobs. The women proving again how industrious and vital they were working on the 'Home Front'.

Songs were popular during those war years that will never be forgotten, here are a few for example. The late Glen Miller's *'Moonlight Serenade'*; and favourite songs for London - *'A Nightingale Sang in Berkley Square'*; *'Roll Out the Barrel'* and *'Yes, We Have No Bananas'*. A rousing moral boosting song - *'There'll Always Be An England'*; then Vera Lynn - affectionately known as the 'Forces Sweetheart', singing two very popular songs - *'We'll Meet Again'* and *'The White Cliffs of Dover'*. Bing Crosby singing - *'White Christmas'* and *'Don't Fence Me In'*, was welcomed by everyone on the Home Front. One of the war's most popular songs was - *'Lilli Marlene'*, and everyone wanted to - *'Hang Out the Washing on the Siegfried Line'*. There were many more songs that live on today that recalls memories of those horrendous war years, some happy memories, but many not so happy!

The War was over and street lights all over Great Britain were switched on illuminating towns and cities that had known nothing but darkness for some six years. The church bells, having been silent through the war years, began to ring out once again over the countryside. Even so, the country suffered austerity for a long time, but the 'Home Front' gradually returned to some normality!

Stanley Naylor

THE HOME FRONT
1939 - 1945
by
Len Cuttler

My Dad was landlord of The Peacock, High Street, Kirton near Boston and I was ten years old and still at school when war was declared in September 1939.

During my time at Kirton School, I cannot remember any truancy at all and seldom were any children late. If a child was absent for any reason, the School Attendance Officer, Mr Russell, soon paid a visit to the child's home to ascertain if the absence was genuine. I think that we were so disciplined in those days that we attended school without question and on leaving school commenced work as a natural progression.

Whilst still attending Kirton School in King Street, evacuees from Hull came to the village in large numbers, in so much that the school could not accommodate them all. This resulted in the Kirton children going to school in the morning and the Hull children in the afternoon, this would be alternated the following week. We enjoyed this arrangement very much, but I am not sure it did our education much good! Gradually a number of the Hull children returned home and our education returned to normal.

I often wonder how the Hull children and their parents coped with the trauma of that time. Some of the families, however, never returned to Hull, their relatives still reside in the village.

In our recreation time, the children of the village would play in the field at the Town Hall where there were swings and a few other amenities. One of the attractions was a large First World War gun, which I and hundreds of other children must have played on over the years. This gun was removed early in World War II and taken for scrap metal, as were many railings.

Kirton School always had a football team for as long as I can remember and the war years were no exception. Mr Frankish, one of the teachers, coached the boys and in 1942 the Kirton team won the Boston Schools league playing such teams as Carlton Road; Staniland; Park Board; St Botolph's; St Thomas's and Tower Road. The winning team members of 1942 were Ron Cartwright (goal keeper); Cecil Clarkson (right back); John Robertson (left back); George Traves (right half); myself (centre half); Norman Taylor (left half); Don Whiley (right wing); Brian Bannister (inside right); Alan Goodley (centre forward); Dave Russell (inside left) and Cliff Neal (left wing). I think as school footballers, we were reasonably good, but our success was partly helped by the fact that we had a number in our team who were above average size.

I cannot say that the members of this winning team went on to further football glory, as few that I remember played much football after leaving school. I had a season or two in Kirton Reserves, but much preferred playing tennis that brought my football career to an end. However, Don Gilliatt, who replaced me in the school team, played for Kirton Town, was spotted by Spalding and went on to play for Boston United as goalkeeper, a position he never played at school, but then injury forced him to retire from the game. In more recent years, the Middlecott School, Kirton, produced a star pupil in Chris Woods, who played goalkeeper for England.

Children were allowed time off school if they wished to work on a farm during the late summer, providing it was to help with what was known at that time as the 'War Effort'. I seem to remember that children had to be twelve years of age and were permitted to work up to three or four weeks. A friend - Derek Fyson and myself did several weeks working for Mr Sid Sizer at Kirton End. We were involved with potato picking, lifting sugar beet, setting plants of varying kinds and at harvest time assisted on the threshing machine. The hours of work were from 8.00am to 4.00pm and the daily pay was 7s.6p. (seven shillings and sixpence - $37^1/_2$p in today's currency). I thought then, and still do, that land work - as it was known - was very hard graft and I made a decision at that time to pursue another career on leaving school.

Therefore in 1943, a few days after my 14th birthday, I commenced my working career as an office boy, joining a staff of thirty at the offices of

W Dennis and Sons Ltd at Kirton House, who had extensive acreage in the district.

One of my duties was writing the names of the farm workers on to time sheets, the numbers must have been in the hundreds plus the foreman on each of sixteen farms. The names of the farms and foremen were written so often that they are imprinted on my mind as follows:-

Bozen Hall (Tom Whitworth); Meers Farm (Jack Taylor); Fishmere End (Bill Taylor); Struggs Hill (Joe Wright); Deans Farm (Albert Hall); Elms Farm (Percy Hall); White House Farm (Fred Goodwin); Lammings Marsh (Jack Cooper); Wyberton Farm (Dick Hall); Manor Farm Frampton (Jack Young); Fosdyke House (Jack Wright); Moulton Seas End (Jack Handbury); Amber Hill (Herbert Hall); Wrangle (Bill Mason); Frithbank (Bill Woods); Gayton-Le-Marsh (Dick Enderby).

I am sure that many local people will remember those individual farms and the foremen of those days. In addition to the farm foremen, Tim Fixter was foreman in charge of the men who worked on the steam cultivators; Len Barlow was in charge of the maintenance garage and Joe Greenfield the foreman in charge of the warehouse near Kirton station.

(This group of farms is an example of the huge farming industry that prevailed during the war years, not just in Lincolnshire, but in other parts of Great Britain. Farmers, with the local workers and the Land Army Girls, helped in the 'Dig For Victory' campaign producing vital food, not just for the 'Home Front', but also for the Armed Forces. Stanley Naylor).

It was a very busy time on the farms during the war years and it was not unusual for the Dennis group of farms to load some forty railway wagons of potatoes a day at Kirton railway station. This was very good business for a small goods station, but it caused an awful lot of frustration to road users when shunting was in progress just at tea-time. The main line gates were closed for long periods causing delays to road traffic that local residents were unable to avoid. Supervising the loading was a well known Kirtonian, Frank Moore and the potatoes were dispatched to various destinations, a large number of them being channelled through the then Ministry of Food.

In 1944 the local potato merchants received an order from the Ministry of Food, to purchase all the potatoes that were available and consign them to the South of England for the first weekend in June. A small, but necessary preparation for the D-Day landings.

We worked many hours during the war. I commenced at 8.30am in the morning (8.00am in the early potato season). Two nights we worked until 6.00pm and three nights until 7.00pm. The main reason for the late nights was because the livestock and farm managers came to the office after tea and John Marshall and myself manned the telephone switchboards. I say switchboards, because there were two, the G.P.O. line and a private telephone system connecting all the farms within a five-mile radius to the office. The private system was fitted with telephones of the type seen in films of the 1920's and 30's, but it worked.

On what I called my 'early' nights, when I finished work at 6.00pm, I then cycled to Boston, a distance of four miles, to attend Night School at Laughton's Buildings. The front cycle light was half covered to comply with the 'Blackout' restrictions in force and as there were no street lights, or lights from anywhere else, they were very dark journeys. It was no use playing truancy from Night School, as Norman Newton, the accountant where I worked, always wanted to see my markings from the previous night. He would assist me with any home work and I have always appreciated his interest in my educational welfare.

On Saturday's we finished work at 1.00pm. It was also pay day and at 12 o'clock, Bill Schofield, the cashier, would give me my week's wages, this being a crisp £1 note. It does not appear much, but my friend, Dave Russell, now living in Canada, informs me that he only received 15/- (15 shillings - or 75p in today's currency) a week in the office of Tunnard Brothers, Station Road, Kirton. So probably I was well paid.

Annual holidays amounted to just one week, supposedly to be taken in arrears. However, this could be negotiated with a sympathetic boss and so the week's holiday could be taken before the year ended.

£5 notes were in circulation during the war and were of the large white coloured kind. These were not often seen, at least not by me and the only time I dealt with such large notes, was when a person came into the office to settle, what was considered at that time, a big bill by cash. The events were so rare that the payer would write their name and address on the back of the £5 note, thus giving it a similar status to that of a cheque.

After a year or so, I lost my office boy status and was promoted to the accounts department. Messrs Dennis's had the most comprehensive and efficient accounting system during those war years and I like to think that I learned a lot during the fifteen years I remained with the company.

In my leisure time I was an active member of the Kirton Tennis Club which was situated down Church Lane and was very successful during the war. This was achieved under the guidance of Mr and Mrs Albert Fyson and Mr Harold Wander. Membership consisted of a number of wives of Kirton men who were in the Armed Forces. Petrol was in short supply so residents were somewhat confined to the village. Nearly every weekend there would be a tennis tournament, members supplied the food that helped to provide local enjoyment in very difficult times. With double summer time in operation, it was not unusual to see tennis played at 10pm. Mrs Muriel Boothby was also a member at that time and with her assistance I have compiled a list of members during the war years as follows:-

Olga Hodges; Marjorie Lucas; Elsie Cox; Frank and Mollie Richer; Phyllis Phoenix; Dick and Madge Upsall; Minnie Headland; Audrey Langdon; Betty Barlow; Joyce Goodwin, Jean Bird; Mary Higgins; Frank Cope; Phyllis Hubbard; Harry and Beatty Foster; Derek Fyson; Percy Pettit; Dr Hardwick; Algy Hills, Sid Smith and myself. Cyril Boothby and Ted Cox were in the RAF and joined in the tournaments when home on leave. My apologies to anyone missed off the list.

(It is worth noting that some of the men in the Club had served in the First World War. Stanley Naylor).

Amongst my varied activities, I was a member of Kirton Army Cadets, a messenger for the Kirton A.R.P. and played for Kirton Brass Band, having joined in 1938.

My first memory actually took place just before the war was declared and it was when members of the Essex Regiment came to Kirton Skeldyke and installed a searchlight battery near the marsh. Transport was in short supply, so undeterred, members walked or cycled the two and half miles once or twice a week to sample the ale at The Peacock.

Names are difficult to recall, but I remember one soldier by the name of Freddie Giltroe who was a very good pianist. He and his fellow comrades would have a good old pub sing song and one of them at that time was 'Three Little Fishes'. Two more soldiers names were Eric Burridge and Dickie Ellis.

At one time during the war, I believe about the time of the D-Day landings, when there was a severe shortage of alcohol, particularly beer, most pubs in the village, and indeed the surrounding district, were only open two or three days a week. It was amazing how the 'Jungle Drums' worked overtime informing everyone that such and such a pub had a delivery on a specific day, thus enabling the drinking fraternity to make a bee-line to the lucky pub!

When the country was preparing for D-Day, there were many troops in this area including the crack paratroopers. There was also a Royal Artillery Mobile Railway Unit which was situated in the railway sidings behind the 'up' platform at Kirton station. It comprised of it's own engine, armoury, cooking unit and living quarters. There was, of course, a huge gun known as 'Big Bertha', capable, we were informed, of firing twenty-six miles. It eventually moved down to the Dover area prior to D-Day.

Food rationing being what it was during the war, schoolchildren and adults could get a mid-day meal at the British Restaurant situated in the premises of the Black Bull on London Road, Kirton. The manageress was Mrs Maud Watkins.

Of the clubs and organisations in the village, Kirton Brass band was one of the first to disband in about 1940, due to the majority of their members joining the forces. According to the Band records this had never happened before since it's formation in 1870. However, the precious instruments were safely stored and shortly after the war ended, the band re-formed and is still going from strength to strength.

The Home Guard was strongly represented in Kirton, their HQ being at the premises of W Dennis and Sons at Kirton House. In command was Mr J G Valentine with the rank of Major, and other officers that I remember were: Capt Dodsworth; Lt Herbert Bird; Lt Jack Holmes; Lt Nev Cooper and Lt Peter Dennis. The Sergeant Major was Ted Smith and Tom Cuttler; Jim Smith; Alf Bevan and Ernie Grooby held the rank of Sergeant.

The Army Cadet Force was formed in the early 1940's and proved extremely popular with the young lads of the district, not least probably because we were issued with an army uniform. The Kirton Platoon trained a couple of times a week and learned the usual skills of map reading, handling rifles, including the firing of them on the rifle range and, of course, marching. We at times joined the Home Guard on exercises and I remember we were useful as 'runners'. We assembled on parade on Sunday mornings, but kept our uniforms on all day because in the evenings a number of us would travel by bus to Spalding to attend the cinema. The main reason for travelling to Spalding was because we qualified for the half price concession operated by the cinema for all persons in uniform. Should any of the cadets be fortunate to make the acquaintance of a young lady, it was hard luck, because there was no time to linger after the picture had ended as the last bus to Kirton left early and no one fancied walking the twelve miles back home.

One useful exercise came from being a member of the cadets was being able to test the gas masks issued to us at the start of the war. We filed through a 'gas chamber' and discovered that the masks actually worked. I seem to remember that the gas was nothing more powerful than tear gas.

Members of the Kirton Platoon I can recall were Peter Usher, Jack Cumberworth, Derek Fyson, Eric Sutton, John Marshall, Dave Russell,

Ken Huskisson, Dennis Palmer, Reg Harwood, Gordon Bedward, Dennis Carter, Jack Neal, Jack Dickinson, Martin Calvert, Eric Rose, Albert Jarvis, Harold Tabor, Len Breathwick, Brian Bannister, Tony Brighton, Joe Bevan, Douglas Burden, Len Warnes, Frank Biggadyke, Roland Eanor and myself. The officers in charge were Lt Alonzo Cantwell and Lt Gordon Wilson. Again my apologies to anyone missed off the list.

One of the finest buildings in the village is the Town Hall, built in 1911 and it played its part in World War II. Each night, a warden and messenger of the ARP (Air Raid Precaution) spent the night in the Hall as also did two nurses. Two bunks were installed for the warden and messenger in what was at that time the Parish Council meeting room and two more for the nurses in the ladies cloakroom at the other end of the building. In the event of a raid and there were several, the messenger had the task of cycling round the village and surrounding area including the Skeldyke over a mile away, to rouse fire fighters at designated houses. Some of the instructions given to a messenger were strange, such as pick up clothes prop at side of garage and knock at second window on the left to waken occupant.

On the nights when there were no raids, card games were played to while away the time. Jesse Webb, who was the night watchman for Tunnard Brothers' warehouse, would cross the road and join in the card game. The warehouse at Tunnard Brothers was formerly a First World War Aircraft Hanger and the site is now occupied by the Primary School.

As a messenger, I welcomed such nights on duty as we were given 7s.6p (seven shillings and sixpence - or $37\frac{1}{2}$ p in today's currency) per night subsistence allowance. This was lot of money in those days when compared to a weekly wage of £1.

After the Dunkirk evacuation in 1940, many troops were billeted in the village. Some were at 'The Grange', London Road (now Parkside) and others in the warehouse located at the rear of Tunnard Brothers Office located on Station Road. On a number of occasions, The Peacock was commandeered as the Officers Mess.

A number of Land Army girls were billeted in 'The Hollies', also on London Road. Like the Hull evacuees, some of them married local men and still live in the area.

The highlight of the week was the Saturday night dance held in the Parish Hall, (the Town Hall being otherwise occupied). The dances were mainly held in aid of the Forces Comforts Fund and the MC was Mr Fred Fossitt, until he too joined the Forces. The doormen were Mr Joe Fox and Mr Ernie Sellars. Bands provided live music including, The Gaiety; The Tuxedoes; Allen and Perkins; Leverton Melody Makers; The Orpheans; Aubrey Woods Trio and a band made up mainly of RAOB members such as Harry Clarke and Wilf Mountain. Village residents, the troops and the Land Army girls supported these dances.

It was in the Parish Hall (now demolished) I was taught my first dance steps by Mrs Eileen Thorne, or as she was then, Eileen Fossitt. The lessons were short lived, as Eileen answered the call of the day and joined the Women's Land Army. She did, however, attend the dances when home on leave.

An amateur dramatic society was formed by one of the evacuee teachers from Hull, Miss Enid Smithers. Shows were performed to capacity audiences in the Parish Hall in aid of Mrs Churchill's Aid to Russia Fund. Artists included Jim and Mrs Morley, Fred Fossitt, Jessie Harvey, Harold Wander, Sid Smith and Dave Russell. Miss Smithers later married a local man, Mr Fred Pinnock and moved away from the district.

Also supporting the War Effort at that time was the Kirton Scouts Group under the leadership of Mr Tom Webb. The Group collected many tons of used paper which was much needed during the war years.

I have only a vague recollection of German POW's, but well remember the Italian POW's arriving in the village. One of them was employed as a stoker at the Gas House on Boston Road. He had quite a lucrative sideline making silver rings out of melted down two-shilling pieces and charging two shillings for his efforts. An entirely accepted illegal business.

Probably one of the most famous people to visit Kirton during the war was Wing Commander Guy Gibson, VC. He was stationed at RAF Coningsby at the time and came to The Peacock on a number of occasions. He was in fact at The Peacock two nights before he was killed.

The 'Blackout' caused many problems and the most important building in the village was the Church, which had difficulty in applying the regulations, not even a chink of light was permissible, this resulted in no evening services. The bells were silent, as I believe they were throughout the country for the duration of the war.

Special Constables played an active part during the war. One of their duties included looking for light shining through blacked out windows. One such Constable was Mr Sherriff Taylor, whose patch covered the Willington Road/Kirton End area. When it was reported to him that a light was shining through the window at the house of Mr Jim Morris, the manager of the Horticultural College, he stated that he would not confront Mr Morris - he wanted to borrow a cultivating harrow from him the next day.

I am sure there are some Kirtonians who will be able to elaborate on my story of what took place in and around the village during those difficult, but interesting war years. But these are my memories and I am sure that similar activities took place in most villages on the 'HOME FRONT'.

I am indebted to my friends, Pete Usher and Dave Russell, for reminding me of certain events and confirming others.

Len Cuttler, 2001

RECOLLECTIONS OF THE SECOND WORLD WAR PERIOD IN KIRTON, BOSTON, LINCOLNSHIRE
by
Colin Cumberworth

As a six-year-old at the outbreak of hostilities, 'politics' was naturally not a normal subject in which I participated - but I was aware of the concern shown by my mother and relatives when war was declared. Having lost two brothers in the 1914/1918 conflict, mother was very concerned as several of our relatives were eligible for 'call-up'.

I recall receiving a small rectangular box with a child-sized gas mask and being instructed how to put it on. There were several designs of gas masks for adults and I still possess one of the brown painted cylindrical metal containers with a fabric lining, used for one type of gas mask. We children were informed of the difference between the wailing of the air-raid siren and the continuance sound of the 'All-clear'.

Although only six years of age - like most children - I quickly became familiar with the names of the aeroplanes of that time and how to recognise them - Bristol Blenheim; Beaufighter; Wellington and, of course, the Hurricane and Spitfire. Soon into the war I was also able to identify many of the German 'planes. Recognition cards etc. were distributed by the Government.

During the period of the war my mother was the landlady of the Great Northern Hotel and we had many soldiers as customers. I was in the unique situation to start a cap badge collection. With hindsight I wish that I had not given my collection away, because the majority of the badges were from Regiments no longer in existence.

The following collection of memories are not in any particular chronological order, but include two large guns in the railway siding behind the 'Up' platform (for passengers boarding trains going south) in Kirton station. They were reputed to have a range in excess of twenty-five miles and were not there for very long, I believe the time would be around 1940/1941.

There was an Ack-Ack Gun emplacement, complete with searchlight, in a field at the back of Mr Neville Cooper's Farm on the Skeldyke Road. The detachment was from the Essex Regiment. The watering-hole for the soldiers was the Great Northern Hotel and quite frequently they would take my sister Greta's cycle - without her knowledge - so they were back on duty within the limit of their allotted free time. PC 'Bill' Riseborough always managed to get the cycle returned safely - until the next time, of course!

One of the 'treats' we looked forward to as children every year was the 'Buffs' tea party. This was held in a variety of places such as the Town Hall, Parish Hall that was in Willington Road, and I recall one occasion it was held in the British Restaurant that is now part of the Black Bull Inn. Local entertainment was often provided, but mainly we had games such as musical chairs. When the party had finished we would all file out and receive a small gift. If the gift included an orange, we thought we had done very well! Oranges were very scarce and bananas were simply unobtainable.

Many leaflets and small books were published during the war with recipes for improvising when certain foods were unobtainable. I well recall my mother making a 'banana spread' from one such recipe with mashed parsnips and banana essence. It was actually better than one expected it to be, but I think I would refuse it if offered today.

Compared with the people living in towns and cities, country dwellers fared much better in respect of food. Cheese, butter, beef and such like products were very scarce for everybody. But at the Great Northern we had a lot of outbuildings and kept chickens that supplied the household with eggs, and fed a pig each year that supplied an abundance of meat. It was the custom at the time to share with other people such things as sausages; pork pies; haslet; pig's fry; braun and scraps. Very few people had refrigerators and domestic deep freezers were unheard of. So the advantage of sharing, was that when recipients of our offerings killed a pig, we received likewise. The bacon joints and hams were 'salted down' (local jargon). 'Putting away' the pig was a highly organised affair and several relatives called in for the day to assist.

The pig-killing season ran roughly from October to March. I frequently watched uncle Charlie Bishop killing pigs in his slaughter house across the road from the Great Northern Hotel. Occasionally I would go with him to farms and cottages in the surrounding villages to kill pigs. Uncle Charlie had a trailer that he towed behind his car that carried a large wooden tub and a type of trolley with two wheels, known as a cratch. The method of killing was with a sharp knife that was inserted into the throat that caused the pig to bleed to death, this would be illegal today. However, Uncle Charlie was an expert and so killing was done very quickly. Only when a pig was reluctant to be restrained would a bolt gun be used, but this method made it difficult to bleed a pig when it was lying down. Thank goodness times have changed!

It was the responsibility of the owner of the pig to provide a substantial amount of hot water that would be poured into the tub. The dead pig would be placed into the hot water to enable the hairs to be scraped off its skin, the hot water also helped to make the skin very white. The carcass relieved of its hair and insides would be hung on a tripod for most of the day to dry.

During the war years I was a member of the 'Servers' at Kirton church and on a Sunday morning would hope the sermon would be short so that I could watch the Home Guard's mock battles or other activities around the village. A real treat was if they were practising throwing Molotov Cocktails in the Hall Weir. An old car would be towed from the end nearest to the junction of Skeldyke Road and Horseshoe Lane towards the far end of the Hall Weir, and then back again. The Home Guard members would light the wick at the end of the bottle and then throw it at the moving target vehicle. This exercise was not carried out too frequently due to the shortage of petrol. It was no coincidence that the exercises managed to finish before the pubs closed at lunchtimes! There was a shortage of beer during the early days of the war and mother tried to share it out amongst the more regular customers. It was necessary, however, to close early some days and occasionally did not open at all.

Living in the Great Northern Hotel enabled me to experience some aspects of the war that most children of my age could not. For example - we frequently received visits from PC Riseborough to inform mother to keep a look out for certain strangers who had been in the area and to let him know immediately if they came in for a drink. Also to listen out for any strange or foreign accents from amongst the customers, or if anyone should ask for information that might have been of use to the Germans. The same directive was given to all the pub landlords in the area. I was told not to answer questions from people I did not recognise. We were also given illustrated posters to display in the bar and taproom with instructions such as 'Careless Talk Costs Lives' and 'Dig for Victory'.

Living so close to the railway station two particular memories are vivid even today. The first concerns the occasion when a German 'plane fired canon shells at a mail train which had just arrived in the station from Peterborough. A recent conversation with Mr Peter Usher (now living in Woodhall Spa) confirmed my own recollection of the event. It took place in either 1940 or 1941. The train arrived in the station at around 0750/0800hrs when the German Heinkel 111K made its first attack. Peter and his sister were in the waiting room beside the platform collecting the daily papers that were being unloaded from the train. It was a cold and misty morning, and on hearing what they thought was gun fire, rushed outside in time to see the 'plane turning to make another attack.

It was probably at that moment that having heard the sound of the 'planes engines, that I managed to get to a bedroom window and saw the Heinkel turn over Craven Avenue positioning itself for a second attack. Fortunately no one was injured and little damage done to the train. Some years later when I was helping to take down a large flag-pole that had become unsafe, that was situated in the garden of the Great Northern Hotel, we discovered one of the canon shells embedded in an old railway sleeper which had been used to support the flagpole. The pole was no more than fifteen yards from our dining room!

The second memory is of a sniper's platform built in one of the trees on the roadside between the Great Northern Hotel and the signal box. A number of horizontal steps had been nailed to the trunk of the tree to give easy access to the platform, which remained in place into the early 1950's. I spent many hours on the platform in the summer months between 1945 and 1950 doing my school homework. A photo can be seen later in the book that was taken just after the war showing the position of the sniper's platform. There is also an aerial photo taken about 1960, after the Great Northern Hotel had been converted into a shop. None of the buildings behind the hotel were there during the war, neither were those in the area between the hotel and the station. This area was arable land filled with fruit trees and vegetable plots.

It is interesting to note that when a local businessman, Mr Frank W Dennis of Frampton Hall, returned from London on the evening express train, it would make an unscheduled stop at Kirton station to allow him to get off. I knew when he was on the train, as his chauffeur would park his car near the signal box that was a few yards up the road from the Great Northern Hotel. Speculation as to why Mr Dennis enjoyed this privilege ranged from a simple ability to pay, to the fact that he may have been a major shareholder in the London and North Eastern Railway, or a combination of both these factors. Whatever the answer, many serving personnel in HM Forces returning home on leave to Kirton - and civilians - had reason to be grateful that Mr Dennis was a fellow passenger, because it enabled them to also get off the train at Kirton, instead of having to travel to Boston.

In 1942 I recall troops and vehicles occupying the Town Hall field, I'm not certain of the Regiment name, but the South Wales Borders comes to mind, and they were only there for a short period of time.

From 1942 onwards I enjoyed cycling down to Kirton marsh, a distance of some three miles, to watch Hurricane and Spitfire fighter aircraft, and later in the war Mosquito fighter/bomber aircraft, practising firing cannon shells at a static target some four to five hundred yards out on the marsh. They approached from the direction of Fosdyke, as the Tornado aircraft do today on their approach to Wainfleet bombing range. There was a large hut built on the bank some 400/500 yards north east of the entrance to Kirton marsh in the direction of Frampton marsh that was manned by the RAF. At both the north east and south west ends of the enclosure surrounding the hut was a mast. Each of these masts had an horizontal spa at the top with an orange coloured lozenge shaped box (i.e. like two pyramids joined at the base) connected to two ropes in the manner of flags. These were used to indicate when practice was about to take place, or was already taking place. This was to warn local fishermen and anyone else on the marsh, of the danger, not just of the shooting, but also of the expended shells falling from the aircraft. I cannot remember the precise combination used, but it was possible to see the boxes from a good distance on the approach to the marsh. Together with friends I would cycle down to Skeldyke to the point where the boxes were visible. If they were indicating that practice was not due to take place, we returned to Kirton and saved an unproductive bike ride. Of course if firing was taking place it was easy to see the 'planes and we would pedal like mad to get to the marsh before firing stopped!

Being close to RAF Coningsby (which was closed for a long period during the war) and other airfields, air activity was always constant. Nevertheless we were always on the lookout for local RAF Pilot, Gordon Ramsey. He would frighten the living daylights out of the local population by flying as low as he dared over the village several times before climbing away with a wave of the wings of the plane. After the war he admitted that on one occasion he thought he would hit the church tower! Gordon took an aerial photograph of the village that has subsequently been used in several articles about Kirton.

Mike Foster was another pilot who would fly over the village. Mike's father, Gilbert Foster, kept the butchers shop (later a branch of the TSB) that was opposite the War Memorial. When Mike returned from a successful bombing raid and his return flight path brought him near to Kirton, he would occasionally fly his 'plane round the village to let his father know he was safe. As a boy I witnessed this event more than once. Thankfully Mike survived the war and was awarded the DFC for bringing his 'plane safely home after being badly damaged. He played for Kirton Cricket Club for a year or two after the war and was a very good batsman, but then he left the district.

On the subject of aeroplanes I think my most vivid recollections concern the fact that from about 1943 the bombing raids to Germany contained an ever increasing number of 'planes. With so many bomber 'dromes sited in North Lincolnshire, one of the normal routes to the continent via Holland to Germany, used Boston as a landmark before heading out over the Wash. Depending where and how far the bombers were going it was certain that from about 8.00pm until 11.00pm, dozens and dozens of bombers would pass over the Kirton and Frampton area, usually flying very low as they struggled to gain height with their very heavy bomb loads. Double summertime meant that even at a very late hour the bombers looked very impressive and menacing silhouetted against the darkening sky. It was rumoured that if they could not reach a certain altitude by the time they reached the Wash they would jettison some of their bombs after they crossed the Norfolk Coast to enable them to gain height. Of course, whilst the sight of these huge bombers heading for Germany was very thrilling for us children, it was perhaps more interesting (if that is an appropriate word) to see many of them coming back at dawn with one or occasionally two engines stopped. There would be smoke or burning oil streaming from the engines, pieces missing from wings and tail, with holes in the body of the plane. As children, we did not appreciate that some of the 'planes would be returning with dead and seriously wounded crew-members. This fact became apparent when my cousin, Denzil Bishop, was reported missing, believed killed in April 1944. No knowledge of the fate of his 'plane has ever come to light.

Kirton was not an obvious target for German bombers but we did have several air raids where incendiary bombs were used. It was suggested that some raids were an attempt by the Germans to set fire to the wheat crops. During such air raids I would look out of the bedroom window and try and make a mental note where the fires were burning (most bombs burned harmlessly in the open fields) and at a later date try and find the stabilising fin off the end of the bomb. On one occasion I discovered an unexploded incendiary bomb which had fallen in the mud at the edge of a pond in a field on the Kirton side of Hunwell House Farm, Frampton, occupied at that time by Mr Dan Goose. Naturally such a trophy had to be taken home! However mother was not pleased and it was promptly placed in a bucket of water. I cannot recall the outcome, but either PC Riseborough or the ARP people removed it. I do know I was not flavour of the month!

Another vivid memory is of the 'Blackout'. It is probably difficult for people born long after the war to appreciate life as we lived it during the war with all the restrictions and shortages and especially the 'Blackout'. Villages, towns and cities without street lights and lights shining from houses. Very few vehicles about at night, and those that were had restricted lighting. Headlamps were fitted with a grill that directed the light downwards which prevented the light shining more than a few yards in front of the vehicle. Cycle headlights were also fitted with an adapter to reduce the forward beam.

Within obvious limitations, those older persons not required for military service, tried to maintain as normal a life for the Kirton residents as possible. Many events were organised to raise money for the war effort. I believe £7000 would provide a Spitfire! For the children fancy dress and decorated cycle competitions were popular. The purchase of National Savings Stamps was encouraged and a book was provided into which the stamps could be saved. Each stamp was of a fairly low cost, perhaps no more than six old pence (2½p in today's currency).

As there was very little traffic on the roads, 'whip and top' was a favourite game with very little danger from cars. I still possess my 'window breaker'. This was a favourite type of 'top'. They were light weight and could be hit - perhaps not always accurately - for quite a distance, hence the name! The game of marbles was popular, usually with glass-alleys, which the older boys would sneak up and try to steal while a game was in progress. Usually they would hand them back, but if they said the words 'Tuzzy-Muzzy' as they picked them off the ground they could keep them!

I cannot recall the Cricket Club operating during the war, but the Bowls and Tennis Clubs were very active. Whist drives were very popular and were organised for raising funds. I don't recall whether dances were popular, as I was too young to be interested!

During the war Jack Hall, his brothers Waples and Teddy, together with Waples' wife, lived in cottages - known as the 'Black Houses' - adjacent to the sea bank down Kirton marsh. They were professional fishermen and owned a fishing-smack called the 'Walmer Castle' that was moored in a creek close to the sea bank. They caught shrimps and raked cockles and mussels according to the season. They also had a flat bottomed boat on which was mounted a punt gun they used for the purpose of wildfowling. The 23rd December 1944 edition of 'Picture Post' featured a two-page article complete with photographs of the brothers wildfowling in the Wash.

Every Wednesday and Saturday, subject to tide times, Jack would make the journey of three and a half miles with pony and trap to deliver fish and fowl to Kirton station destined for London markets, and collect provisions from the village shops. He would keep strictly to his route around the village, which the pony grew to know and the last port of call on the way home was the Great Northern Hotel. The pony would automatically stop at the front door and would not continue on its journey until Jack had collected some bottles of beer! Occasionally I would initially make the journey back to the cottage with Mr Hall and stay for tea, my brother, also named Jack, would collect me taking me home on the crossbar of his cycle. Later when I had a cycle of my own, a space would be found for it in the trap.

Prior to the recent closure of the marsh footpaths because of the foot-and-mouth problem, I regularly walked the sea bank and always stopped at the site where the cottages stood, long since demolished, to reflect on times gone by. Only two old apple trees remain with a few snowdrops here and there. Ploughing in the field adjacent occasionally reveals broken china, otherwise there is little evidence of former occupation.

Early in the war years, a concrete barrier was erected at the Stag and Pheasant corner between the hairdresser's shop and Fossitt and Thorne's former cycle shop. The idea was to create a road hazard in case of invasion. Sadly a jeep travelling from the direction of Boston carrying American servicemen failed to negotiate the hazard and a serious accident occurred. I cannot remember if there were any fatalities.

We are accustomed today to seeing very large commercial vehicles on our roads, but during the war there was great excitement amongst the children if what was known as a 'sixty-footer' passed through the village, or even better one should stop to give the driver a break. They were RAF 'plane transporters known in the service as 'Queen Mary's'. They frequently carried the remains of German aircraft, which had been shot down. We eagerly looked for bullet and cannon shell holes and were not averse to try and pinch a souvenir. The debris had a peculiar smell of oil and rubber that I will never forget.

I have memories of horses hauling sugar beet to Kirton station and one of them bolted off the ramp at the King Street end and was killed. Of buses towing a gas-making device. The Kirton Girl Guides making a 'Penny Trail' around the wall of the War Memorial for the 'Poppy Appeal' fund. Mr Frankish giving magic lantern slide shows at the school, and putting $1/3$ pint bottles of milk in front of the fire at the junior school to warm for drinking mid-morning. Ice skating in the winter on the Hall Weir and the 'Lows', a pit between the Meers and Fishmere End. Then I'll never forget the horrible tasting margarine!

During the war years Kirton was of course much smaller in terms of population than at the present time. New houses have been built on Edinburgh Estate, Dennis Estate and Marketstead Estate, plus other private developments. Several well known landmarks have disappeared, the Great Northern Hotel for example that was demolished to make way for Pell's Drive. Others include The Grange at Marketstead, Tunnard's Hanger in Station Road and the station itself was demolished to make way for the new road.

Other landmarks have taken on another identity. Well known pubs, The Kings Head and The Kings Arms in the village, The Windmill at Kirton End and The Boat and Gun in Skeldyke are private houses. Captain Rolff was in charge of the former Church Army Social Centre in Sutterton Road, that is now Fossitt and Thorne's main tyre depot.

Only a few of the businesses operating during the war have survived. The only two not to have changed names are Jessops the Bakers and the Co-op, the latter having changed location. G B and A Deaton, Gents' Hairdressers, formally Len Taylor and during the war was owned by the well-known Joe Morley. Mr Sampson's chemist shop has changed names but is still a chemist. Storey's butcher's shop has also changed names but remained butchers. Miss East's corner shop has changed names but remains a sweet and paper shop.

Shops and businesses that were part of the Kirton I knew during the war years include W Wander - Grocer; 'Saddler' Marshall - Saddler; Gilbert Foster - Butcher; Harry Woods - Shoemaker (best known as 'Cobbler Woods'). 'Bloggy' Fox - Cycle Shop; Mr Boyce - Plumber and Decorator; Tunnard's Garage that was on the site of the library and NatWest Bank, later moved to the site of the Grange under the name of Baitstrands Garage, now Landrover. Dickens - Bakers; Kents - Corn Merchants; 'Clockey Harris' - Watch repairer; Sid Bannister - Tailor; Tommy Webb - Tailor; Baxter and Guion - Potato Merchants; Fred Fossitt - Greengrocer; Sid Smith - Poultry Farmer and Teddy Flower - Blacksmith.

These are some of my recollections of the war years as a boy of six to eleven years of age.

Colin Cumberworth, 2001

Postscript:

I notice in my brother Jack's war recollections that he mentions a soldier playing a piano accordion in the Great Northern Hotel, to which I can add the following:

When the soldier was posted away from Kirton he left the accordion with my mother for safekeeping. Several years after the war we had not heard from him and assumed that he had not survived. However, Wilfred Pickles of 'Have A Go' fame, had another radio programme entitled I believe 'Where Are You Now'. My sister, Greta Chaplin, wrote a letter to Wilfred Pickles about the fact that our mother was still in possession of the accordion. The letter must have been well composed because Wilfred read it out on the radio in its entirety. Someone recognised the soldier's name and description, and to our great joy and satisfaction both soldier and accordion were re-united.

Another similar situation occurred concerning some photograph albums, which I was aware of, having looked at them when the soldier, Bill

Rootes was posted to the Far East. The albums were left at the Great Northern Hotel for safekeeping and, although we knew his name, we did not know if he had survived the war, or even knew his home address.

Over the years the albums were forgotten and did not come to light until my sister, brother and myself were going through our mother's effects after she died in 1981. I then decided that I must try and find Bill Rootes, or at least his next of kin. Bill was a regular soldier and a drummer in a band at the outbreak of World War II. Most of the photographs were of army parades in India, and a close examination of one of them with a magnifying glass revealed on one of the drums the name of the Gloucestershire Regiment.

I then wrote to the Regiment Museum in Gloucester to see if they knew of the whereabouts of Bill Rootes. To my delight he had survived the war - although his opinion of the Japanese could not be printed here - and was an active member of the Gloucestershire Regimental Association living in Corringham, Essex. It was my pleasure to personally be able to return the albums to the rightful owner, who had forgotten where he had left them. Sadly Bill died a few years ago, but at least he was reunited with his albums.

Colin Cumberworth

"Never in the field of human conflict was so much owed by so many to so few".

Winston Churchill referring to the courage of the Battle of Britain pilots in August 1940.

WARTIME MEMORIES - 1939 to 1945
by
Jack Cumberworth

My memories of the war years include the two 9.2 Howitzer Guns being in the siding behind the platform at Kirton station.

Of joining the Air Cadets and being in their bugle band. One highlight was playing on stage at the Odeon cinema in Boston at a big charity concert to raise money for the RAF.

I then joined the Kirton contingent of Army Cadets, and remember being with the Cadets and Home Guard on manoeuvres in the park at Sutterton, when there was a daylight raid over Boston. The Home Guard manned Lewis Machine Guns during the period of the raid.

From the age of fourteen years until I joined the Army at seventeen years and a half, I was an Air Raid Messenger. I'm not sure that being on duty with Mr Dean Tunnard had anything to do with a well known fact there were no Air Raids when we were on duty. I only called out the Wardens once in three and a half years, and that was at the end of my service.

Austerity buses with Gas-bags on the roof were seen regularly. Then there was the sniper position built in a tree near the Great Northern Hotel.

A German 'plane was forced down somewhere in the Sibsey area north of Boston. It was reputed at the time that the pilot asked if there was a Mr John Taylor in the area. Apparently before the war the pilot had done business with John Taylor, who was a well-known potato merchant from Gosberton, and later of Kirton.

One day I was standing at the station gates when Harold (Kipper) Franks was on his way for an interview to join the RAF as a Rear-Gunner. He was asking himself mental questions on arithmetic, at the same time he was asking me if his answers were correct.

There was a Land Mine dropped on Marshall Bannister's land, that I'm sure was known as the Hunwell, that made a huge crater.

One peculiar phenomenon that I experienced during those war years, was that normally I was a heavy sleeper and needed to be shaken to be awakened. But if there was an Air Raid imminent, or even if German planes were in the area, I was awakened by the mooing and agitation of cows in the field on the opposite side of the road to the Great Northern Hotel behind Uncle Charlie's house. The field was known as Gash's field, and strangely the cows would often be disturbed long before we heard the Air Raid Siren.

I had a fear of being in the house should it be bombed, so always got-up and went outside during an Alert. On one occasion on a moonlight night, I saw a RAF Night Fighter chasing a German Bomber, and I believe the German was shot down over the marshes. On another occasion the cows were very agitated when thousands of incendiary bombs were dropped in the area, intended for the harvest crops. It was shortly after this raid that my brother, Colin, brought home a live incendiary bomb that was promptly placed in a bucket of water, but I don't recall what happened to it.

After closing time at the Great Northern Hotel, my mother, who was the landlady, would entertain the soldiers playing the piano and singing songs, one soldier would join in playing an accordion.

The Searchlight Unit positioned in Mr Neville Cooper's field down the Skeldyke Road, was quite at attraction for me, and most enjoyable when I was allowed to sit in the observers' chair.

My cousin, Denzil Bishop was an RAF Bomber Pilot, sometimes on training flights he would fly over Kirton, buzzing his grandmother's house (Mrs Flatters). Sadly he was lost on a bombing raid without trace. His brother, Major Bub Bishop, was for some years the Marshall at the Kirton Armistice Parade.

I hope my brief memories are of interest and show to some degree how we lived as teenagers through the war years.

Jack Cumberworth, 2001

A Wartime Childhood In Lincoln
by
Maureen Street

The experiences of a small child growing up are frequently traumatic, but wartime Lincoln made it more so. In fact, about my first memory was of a factory woman being killed by a convoy. The heavy roar of advancing vehicles was getting louder and louder. Standing on tiptoe I peered through the front-room window. On her bicycle was a young woman in a turban returning from a munitions factory. Then she was gone - for ever - as the convoy roared by. Under the quaking leaves of the sycamore trees remained a tarpaulin-covered mound - just the rim of a bicycle wheel showing. Fortunately I had a loving mother to put her arms around me. She was one of many mothers who remained at home making ends meet - 'making do and mending' as best she could. But she always seemed to be crying - her head buried in her hands.

'You'll know when I'm better, I shall be singing!' And sing she did. The months had seemed endless until up the steps she went and whitewashed the pantry - 'Whiter than the whitewash on the wall' and 'We'll be hanging out the washing on the Siegfried Line', were her favourites.

However, spells of depression lasted until the end of the war, when she was referred to the local big psychiatric hospital high above South Common at Bracebridge Heath, Lincoln. There she had ECT twice a week and came back with tales of toilet doors covering only half the doorway, but also I have wonderful pictures of her recovering on the balcony in the sunshine after her ECT.

War or no war, children had to be brought up and she taught me how to read and write. On her knee I was taught three letters of the alphabet each week from the back page of 'Tiny Tots' comic. She also made a ball from strips of inner tubing placed on top of each other; with this I played ball games against the air raid shelter wall at the end of the passage.

Some houses down the street had an Anderson shelter dug out in the back yard. As our house was on a slope, however, we had a steel table shelter installed. What better place for a pretend lions' cage or a stage for noisy tap dancing in shoes with studs in - another economy measure for conserving the leather. I used to run along to the cobblers at the corner shop for a piece of leather. After hacking out the shape of the sole Grannie used to nail it to my little shoes on the hobbing iron.

Occasionally, my baby brother was trundled along in the pram to the WVS Centre at Clashet Gate. I trotted along at the side, holding onto the brake. "New" shoes! They turned out to be ill-fitting and pinched a bit, but Grannie soon produced a sharp knife from her battered old handbag and made a nick in them. Then the rumour went round that drinking chocolate had come in from Canada. You only had to take an empty jar - they said. Then we were asked to collect rosehips for syrup, they gave us a threepenny bit for a jarful.

Then there was the requirement to use spare rooms for evacuees, service personnel and civilians. One evening there was a heavy knock at our front door. A police sergeant wanted my mother to become a landlady and take in a constable. At that time there was no choice. Jack Lacey had had most of his biceps shot away at Dunkirk and was no further use for active service. He was like a big brother and we adored him, trying on his helmet and keeping a lookout for the warning flashing light at the corner, which indicated that he must ring up the police station. With lots of encouragement, we massaged his balding head and even washed his tired feet when he came in. It was then that he would bury his head in his hands at thoughts of the mass exodus from Dunkirk and those who hadn't survived.

Despite our limited rather ragged text-books I loved to go to school, where my favourite teacher was black-haired Miss Guzzeloni, who wore a cream sprigged smock. Her hair was tucked in a roll round an old stocking wound round her head. Brer Rabbit was the favourite story - the one with the tar baby. She used to lead us in singing 'Ten green bottles' in the air raid shelter. However, her mind must have been far away in war-torn Italy where she returned after the war, scouring the ravaged Abruzzi area for lost starving children who roamed around in gangs. The role of our school was to collect bars of chocolate to send to them.

Lincoln was lucky in escaping the worst of the German bombs, but we did have one bomb. One Sunday, mother had just laid the table when the siren went. Under the table she dived and tea stains appeared all over the cloth. That was the occasion of Lincoln's only bomb. The convalescent home was destroyed as was the boarding house of the High School just below the Cathedral. Two mistresses were killed and fifteen girls.

At Lincoln, children continue to go to school with dinners provided and a third of a pint of milk at playtime. We also returned in the holidays to receive our allocation of milk. The country's children had to be kept healthy. We would gather round the field kitchen in the playground playing at mothers and fathers. Our generation of children only recognised bananas from a cut out picture on the shop window opposite the school. In the absence of sweets - a stick of cinnamon or a stick of liquorice. The doll whose head I had broken mysteriously reappeared at Christmas with a golden yellow outfit and brown mending wool plaits. Undressed she had the familiar ABC on her front and 123 on her back!

Before Christmas, my father had taken me on a bus with wooden slatted seats into the country. It was blackout and inky dark when we got out at the village of Bassingham. We stepped out into a gloomy cottage, lit by an oil lamp illuminating dark oil paintings hanging on the low walls. Then two feathered chickens were handed to my father. There they hung at my father's side - our Christmas feast! Then back on the bus to Lincoln.

For the next six months mother somehow saved her points or coupons to buy tinned puddings and corned beef to take on our holiday to Mablethorpe on the east coast. The weight on my father's shoulders! Along the front a patch of beach the size of a tennis court had been cleared of mines and surrounded by barbed wire. There we played in the sand but could only look at the sea.

All over the country every scrap of metal from gates, railings and playgrounds was removed to smelt down for guns. There was precious little left to play with. But nothing could take away our imaginations. In local Abbey grounds the exposed roots of two centuries-old trees became our play homes and we sang and jumped and brushed up with bundles of twigs. We skipped and chanted traditional children's rhymes.

Occasionally we would hear the siren on top of a wooden framework at the end of the school. Down the cellar we would go, crouching in the tiny space under the stairs. Sometimes my baby brother would cry and I would be frightened that the enemy would hear him at the top of the chimney. A newspaper cartoon in the News Chronicle of a jackboot coming down on top of a baby lying on the ground also terrified me.

And what were my reactions when the war came to an end? One evening my mother called up the stairs, "The war is over!" She had nobody else to tell - my father was on nights at the munitions factory. I felt that something should happen, but it didn't, so I went to sleep.

Maureen Street

(Reproduced from 'Civilians At War' by permission of the publishers - Change Charity)

THE SIREN SONG

There goes the Siren,
Oo - Oo - Oo,
Here comes the Jerry bomber,
What is he going to do?
Off to the shelter away we must go,
Wait for the "All Clear" to blow.
Oo - Oo - Oo

Children in the second standard at St Mary's School, Boston, sang the above ditty when in the air-raid shelter. Boston Guardian 29th January 1941.

WERE YOU AT DUNKIRK?

Were you there that fateful summer?
    When the whole world held its breath?
When the whole world gazed in wonder
    At an army facing death?
When it seemed as though a mighty host
    Would live to fight no more
Till the small ships and the tall ships
    Brought them safe to England's shore?

Many thousand tides have risen
    Over Dunkirk's shores since then
But we'll not forget the story
    Though a million rise again.
Were you there that fateful summer?
    When a nation knelt in prayer?
Then be proud all you who answer
    'I was there - yes, I was there'.

© *Victor Cavendish 1981*

THE HOME GUARD ON PARADE

(This story has been gleaned from the Boston Guardian newspaper dated May 1943. It depicts, however, a Parade of the Home Guard that could so easily have taken place in many parts of the British Isles and most likely did! See photograph later in the book) *S.N.*

Fine Demonstration at Boston

Three years ago the Home Guard was formed. It was ill equipped and all too often the personnel suffered the sniggers of some who saw them drill.

Sunday saw the local Home Guard parade in Boston equipped with modern weapons of war. They were no longer raw material, but a big assembly of thoroughly efficient men going through their paces with precision worthy of regulars, all exhibiting the efforts of many hours of vigorous and exacting drill in what otherwise would have been leisure time.

Some thousands of people watched an impressive display in the Central Park and there were no scoffers. Everyone was full of unstinted admiration for a fine body of men.

The huge concourse of spectators included the Mayor and Mayoress, Councillor and Mrs. G.H. Bird; the deputy-Mayor and deputy-Mayoress, Councillor and Mrs. J.G. Wrigley; Colonel Luker, D.C.M., M.C., Zone Commander; Councillor W.E. Anderson, Chief Warden; Mr. Jasper Sharpe, deputy Chief Warden; and officers of the Home Guard.

Prior to the proceedings Captain and Adjutant Mothersole explained some details of the intention of the parade.

IN GREATEST PERIL

Lieutenant - Colonel O.B. Giles, in the course of a short speech reminded the assembly that they were commemorating the third anniversary of the formation of the Home Guard. The Prime Minister had expressed the hope that wherever possible they should mark the occasion by giving displays to let the public know what they were doing.

Three years ago England stood in the greatest peril in her history. Denmark, Norway, Holland, Belgium and France had been or were being over-run by the strongest and best-equipped Army in the world. A fortnight afterwards the British Army, having lost its tanks, guns and equipment had been evacuated from Dunkirk and we were standing alone. The Prime Minister had taken office on 12 May - an office of great and terrible responsibility. By his spirit of undaunted determination and courage he had given the British people new hope, resolved to fight on whatever the cost and whatever the odds.

On 14 May 1940, the Government decided to form a citizen army of Local Defence Volunteers. Afterwards they were renamed by the Prime Minister as the Home Guard.

FIRST DIFFICULTIES

Within a few days hundreds and thousands of loyal British people old and young, were rallying to the Defence Volunteers and within a week they were manning posts throughout the length and breadth of England. From shore to shore they were on guard - in the towns, cities, villages, on the coast, on the hills and in the fens.

They were a motley crowd, some with caps and some with armlets, some had rifles, some even had pikes. Whether they were armed or not, they were equipped with one resolve and that was to fight to the last against any invader and to defend their country, their homes and their freedom.

That day, three years after, they had a Home Guard nearly two million strong, properly clothed and equipped and armed with all kinds of modern weapons and they also had the necessary ammunition. They had rifles, Sten guns, Lewis guns, machine guns, armoured cars, bombs, grenades and anti-tank guns.

Now that the Regular Army was fighting overseas, the Home Guard had added responsibility in the defence of England. It was their duty to keep alert, fully trained and efficient and their task would not be done until they had defeated Hitler and his Nazi hordes. The enemy was still strong and capable of unexpected acts, but if he came the Home Guard would do its duty.

FINE DEMONSTRATION

Then followed, for an hour, a most interesting demonstration dealing with every branch of Home Guard activity, including the use of various types of weapon, from rifles to guns of larger calibre.

The large crowd was intensely interested in actual firing and although rubber projectiles were used in place of bombs and grenades, it was not difficult to imagine what damage would have been done by explosive missiles.

In a central position was a dummy tank and the crowd had the advantage of seeing 'bombs' and anti-tank projectiles being fired at it. When a direct hit was scored the applause was enthusiastic.

Captain Motherwell gave a lucid explanation of every type of action taken. The delight of the crowd was considerable when, at the cessation of firing, two of the 'enemy' crew made an unexpected appearance from the interior of the tank, exhibiting a white flag and with hands upraised!

The demonstration was most heartening. It showed beyond a shadow of doubt how well equipped is the Home Guard today and how efficient are its members. They started from scratch, but today they are a fine body of men, well trained, well equipped and with unbounded enthusiasm. Hats off to them.

Produced from the Boston Guardian 1943 by permission of The British Library.

In the years when our Country was in mortal danger

HORACE R. CHAMBERS

who served 22/6/42 to 31/12/44

gave generously of his time and powers to make himself ready for her defence by force of arms and with his life if need be.

George R.I.

THE HOME GUARD

THE BRITISH RESISTANCE ORGANISATION
1940 to 1944
by
Stanley Naylor

During my tour of duty in France in 1944/45 as a driver with 2831 Squadron RAF Regiment, I was privileged to meet at least a couple of the French Resistance and learned first-hand of some of their exploits. Then many years later on tours of the First World War battlefields on the Somme, I saw the grimmest place in Arras that relates to the Second World War. This is the Mur des Fusilees with its execution post and 200 plaques forming the memorial to the French patriots that were executed between 1941 and 1944. This was the French underground movement known as the Maquis.

Therefore, I am fully aware of the enormous risk that was taken by each and every one who volunteered to form local groups of resistance. Although they wore ill fitting khaki uniforms and operated under the umbrella of the Home Guard, their roll was entirely different.

I am indebted to the sprightly eighty-six year 'young' Eddie Welberry for the information on the British Resistance Organisation on which I have based this story.

It was after the evacuation of Dunkirk in 1940 when we were vulnerable to an invasion, that Winston Churchill decided to form a secret underground army code-named 'Auxiliary Units' under the leadership of Colonial Colin Gubbins, later to become Sir Colin Gubbins. So the British Resistance Organisation (BRO) was born and likely recruits were vetted by Special Branch Officers and duly signed the Official Secrets Act. They were then informed they had been selected for special Home Guard duties and was joining one of the three battalions that covered the country, Lincolnshire being 202 Battalion. Because they were never officially registered as being members of the Home Guard and therefore enrolled as fighting men, the question arises whether they were strictly covered by the Geneva Convention of July 27th 1929. We were afforded that protection as members of HM Forces, if captured we were only required to give name, rank and number and not to impart any further information. We know, of course, that Germany and Japan ignored that protection for many POW's. What then would have been the fate of members of the British Resistance Organisation had Germany invaded our Island and they had been captured? The Home Guard uniform may have only afforded short term protection!

Therefore no stone was left unturned to find the right men for this hazardous, but vital job of causing as much disruption to an invading force as possible. They were highly trained, not to confront the enemy, that was the roll of the Home Guard to defend our shores and a great job the HG would have done had an invasion took place, in spite of all the jokes and banter about 'Dad's Army'.

The BRO's roll was to hide in their cells until the enemy was established then emerge at night and disrupt communications and supplies and disappear under the cover of darkness. A cell comprised of five or six men with an underground hideout that was stocked with provisions to last them at least two or three weeks. It may have been possible for them to live at home during the day, as most of them would have been in reserved occupations, even though their family were not aware of the secret task they had undertaken. Mrs Jessie Welberry remarked during my interview with Eddie, how his clothes smelled musty after a night on duty, as she assumed it was with the Home Guard, but no doubt it was spent in a hideout with no air-conditioning. See the story later in the book on a good friend, the late Fred Fossitt and the reason for his red face, proving again the secrecy of the operation!

Age was no barrier for recruits who were drawn from all walks of life. Ideally they were farmers, gamekeepers - even poachers and wild-fowlers, all familiar with their own particular part of Great Britain. So secret were these Auxiliary Units that they did not know who occupied adjoining cells that dotted the countryside.

I was amazed to learn that Auxiliary Units had high priority to weapons and explosives. For example they were provided with the Thompson sub-machine-gun that was far superior to the Sten gun we used, also plastic explosives and certain delay mechanisms, before they were available to the Forces. They had use of the 36M (Mills) hand grenade, this was standard issue to us that we knew as the 'pineapple', because of its shape. The Auxiliaries were issued with various other weapons including the Fairburn Commando dagger and some experimented with bows and arrows, both weapons useful for silent killing, especially at night.

Incendiary devices included a Magnesium Incendiary, a No. 76 Grenade (A W Bottle) and a Pocket Time Incendiary, all needed to be handled with care, but very efficient for practical use.

Just to give an indication of the weapons and ammunition that was available to the Auxiliary Units, these details have been taken from 'The Last Ditch' by David Lampe (details later).

Mr Reginald Sennitt was in charge of a nucleus of cells, perhaps five or six and when the Auxiliary Units were stood down in 1944 all the weapons and ammunition was collected from these cells and stored at Mr Sennitt's farm. The Army, however, forgot about Mr Sennitt and with secrecy being uppermost in his mind he was unable to confide in anyone. Then in 1964 he threw caution to the wind and notified local police of the contents of his shed.

The police in turn notified the Army and on 7th April 1964, Staff Sergeant R Sibson of the Royal Army Ordnance Corps compiled this inventory.

14,738 rounds of ammunition for pistols, rifles and sub-machine guns, including a quantity of incendiary bullets.

1,205 lb of gelignite, of Noble 808 and of plastic explosive, most of it in a safe enough condition to take away.

3,742 ft delayed action fuse;

930 ft instantaneous safety fuse;

250 ft detonating cord;

1,447 time pencils;

1,207 L-delay switches (a later form of time pencil which, instead of relying on acid, is triggered by induced metal fatigue);

719 push, pull and pressure release booby-trap switches;

314 paraffin bombs and

340 igniters for these bombs and for the safety fuses;

131 fog signals;

121 smoke bombs;

212 thunderflashes;

571 primers;

36 1-lb slabs of gun cotton;

4 hand grenades;

10 phosphorous grenades;

33 time-pencils and booby trap switches attached to made-up charges.

Multiply this arsenal by the number of Auxiliary groups up-and-down the country and we had a formidable under-cover Resistance Organisation that would, without any shadow of a doubt, have done an awful lot of damage to an invading enemy.

Membership of the BRO had grown to such an extent in 1942 that it was decided to issue a Training Manual, but it needed to be camouflaged and this was on the cover:

THE COUNTRYMAN'S DIARY 1939

DO THEIR STUFF UNSEEN
UNTIL YOU SEE
RESULTS

With the Compliments of:
    HIGHWORTH & CO.

<u>YOU WILL FIND THE NAME HIGHWORTH</u>
<u>WHEREVER QUICK RESULTS</u>
<u>ARE REQUIRED</u>

Training in gorilla warfare continued and the hideout at Swineshead, known as an OB (Operational Base) had six volunteers, one of whom was Eddie Welberry. Other hides were at Kirton, Butterwick, Quadring, Holbeach and Crowland, just to name a few of the thirty/thirty five that was established in Lincolnshire and of nearly a thousand that was constructed around the British Isles.

Eddie informed me that siting was critical, access hatches had to be absolutely concealed, as also had the separate exit, which was just as important as the entrance. Sites were in woodlands, under derelict farm buildings, in disused mines, under wood piles and various other weird places. Damp was minimised by concealed ventilation, but modern air-conditioning would have eradicated the mustiness that prevailed. Contents of an OB included wooden tables, benches and bunk beds, paraffin heaters and lamps, hence the reason for adequate ventilation, there were storage lockers and a chemical toilet. There was also a bottle of rum included on the inventory, but for what purpose, medicinal or moral?

Some Auxiliary Units constructed their own OB's, but the Royal Engineers took over the bulk of the work aided by specialist civilian contractors, the latter having no idea what they were building. Some sites were accidentally discovered that were abandoned and new sites were subsequently found.

The British Auxiliary Units gained immense knowledge from the experience of the European Resistance Movement that gave them a head start. They were highly trained, well organised and fully supplied with necessary materials for effective sabotage of enemy supply lines. Although small in numbers, they would have been in a prime position to recruit and train new members. Unfortunately though, they would have suffered from the activities of collaborators and informers, as did their counterparts in France and other occupied countries. Even so, the high calibre of these men would have seen those remaining carry on the sabotage activities, regardless of any lurking dangers.

All the women who were able joined almost every organisation on the Home Front and did a marvellous job, but I have not found any sign of one of them joining a local Resistance Group. However, a group of ATS

Officers were assigned to the Organisation to operate a secret communication network within the BRO. This small group of young women would have been vital to the Resistance workers, had the enemy been allowed to invade our island.

Then after 'D' Day in June 1944 the war situation changed, the threat of invasion had passed and in November that year it was decided that the Auxiliary Units should stand down. Unfortunately, because of the secret nature of their duties, it was not possible at that time to receive public recognition, therefore these two letters are of vital importance to each of them. They have been copied from originals kindly loaned to me by Eddie Welberry.

The Commander,
<u>GHQ Auxiliary Units.</u>

In view of the improved war situation, it has been decided by the War Office that the Operational Branch of Auxiliary Units shall stand down and the time has now come to put an end to an organisation which would have been of inestimable value to this country in the event of an invasion.

All ranks under your command are aware of the secret nature of their duties. For that reason it has not been possible for them to receive publicity, nor will it be possible even now. So far from considering this to be a misfortune, I should like all members of Auxiliary Units to regard it as a matter of special pride.

I have been much impressed by the devotion to duty and high standard of training shown by all ranks. The careful preparations, the hard work undertaken in their own time and their readiness to face the inevitable dangers of their role, are all matters which reflect the greatest credit on the body of picked men who form the Auxiliary Units.

I should be glad, therefore, if my congratulations and best wishes could be conveyed to all ranks.

(Signed) H E Franklyn

GHQ Home Forces, General
18th November 1944 Commander-in-Chief

                Pte E Welberry
From: Colonel F W R Douglas
To: The Members of Auxiliary Units - Operational Branch

The War Office has ordered that the Operational side of Auxiliary Units shall stand down! This is due to the greatly improved War situation and the strategic requirements of the moment.

I realise that joining Auxiliary Units has meant to you; so do the officers under my command. You were invited to do a job which would require more skill and coolness, more hard work and greater danger, than was demanded of any other voluntary organisation. In the event of 'Action Stations' being ordered you know well the kind of life you were in for. But that was in order; you were picked men and others, including myself, knew that you would continue to fight whatever the conditions, with, or if necessary without, orders.

It now falls to me to tell you that your work has been appreciated and well carried out and that your contract, for the moment, is at an end. I am grateful to you for the way you have trained in the last four years. So is the Regular Army. It was due to you that more divisions left this country to fight the battle of France; and it was due to your reputation for skill and determination that extra risk was taken - successfully as it turned out - in the defence arrangements of this country during that vital period. I congratulate you on this reputation and thank you for this voluntary effort.

In view of the fact that your lives depended on secrecy no public recognition will be possible. But those in the most responsible positions at General Headquarters, Home Forces, know what was done; and what would have been done had you been called upon. They know it well, as is emphasised in the attached letter from the Commander-in-Chief. It will not be forgotten.

                                            (Signed by the Colonel)

30 Nov 44 Colonial
c/o GPO HIGHWORTH Commander
Nr. Swindon (Wilts) Auxiliary Units

In 1997 and dedicated to all Auxiliary Units, the British Resistance Organisation Museum was opened on part of Parham Airfield, Framlingham, Suffolk. There is a unique display of memorabilia and further information can be obtained from: Colin Durrant, 101 Avondale Road, Ipswich, Suffolk, 1PS 9LA.

Also the Government has bestowed public recognition on members of the Auxiliary Units by awarding them the 1939 - 1945 Defence Medal. This was not possible when they disbanded in 1944 because of the strict secrecy of the organisation and also because they were not registered as members of HM Forces.

The Defence Medal was awarded to all those of us who were in the HM Forces and served in the UK during the years of World War II. I for one, therefore, are pleased that this group of stalwart volunteers, who gave up their free time to train to extremely high standards and was prepared to thwart an invasion of an enemy, has now public recognition. May they never be forgotten!

Acknowledgement

Eddie Welberry gave me most of this story, but I acknowledge that some material came from **THE LAST DITCH** by David Lampe and published by Cassell of London in 1968, that gives a detailed account of this secret organisation. The book is highly commended but maybe out of print, however, copies are available in libraries.

Stanley Naylor

Here's the reason for red face 27 years ago

LAST week's front-page story in the "Standard" about British "Resistance" groups in Lincolnshire has removed a 27-year-old embarrassment for Mr. Fred Fossitt, of Westfield House, Willington Road, Kirton.

In 1941, he was Company Sergeant Major Fossitt, of the secret underground army — but his wartime role was so secret that it let him in for a very embarrassing experience.

Like the other Lincolnshire men secretly trained as resistance fighters in the event of occupation of Britain by the Germans in the 1939-45 war, Mr. Fossitt was then (as he is now) a well-known local personality. Among other things, he was secretary of the Forces' Benevolent Fund, set up in the village to make gifts to local boys and girls in the Services.

BIG SEND-OFF

But as a specially-trained underground fighter he knew he would not be called up as they had been. The secret training given to the British "Resistance" how to use all kinds of weapons, from revolvers to machine guns; how to move like shadows, and kill with knives and bare hands; and how to handle all types of explosives. So when he was called up into the Army in August, 1941, Mr. Fossitt knew it would not be for long, as his skills were needed at home.

He could not tell anyone that, however—and the Benevolent Fund Committee was resolved to give its secretary a good send-off.

In spite of his protests, and because he could not given any reason for them, a big dance was organised with him as guest of honour, and the proceeds were formally presented to him. Scores of people called to say goodbye — and within four days, Mr. Fossitt was back home and apparently a civilian again

CLEARS MYSTERY

"It was all very embarrassing," Mr. Fossitt smiled this week. "I gave the money to the Red Cross, but it was a long time before I got over the feeling of having been a fraud in taking it, when I knew all the time that I would not be kept in the army. Still, I couldn't tell anybody how I felt. Even after all these years, I hope anyone who remembers it will now understand .. "

For his family, the book* about the British "Resistance Movement" recently published clears up another little mystery. A day came in 1944 when Mr. Fossitt received two letters in one week. One was addressed to C.S.M. Fossitt (it was a certificate of merit, thanking him for his special services). The other was addressed to Private Fossitt. It was his long-postponed call-up.

COUNTY BOWLER

After service in Palestine with the explosives section of the Ordnance Corps, Mr. Fossitt returned to Baxter and Guion Ltd., the agricultural produce firm he has been with for 38 years. He is now a director of the firm, and as a potato merchant is a former president of the South Lincolnshire Wholesale Potato Merchants Association, and is currently vice-president of the National Joint Council of British Potato Merchants.

He has always played an active part in the community life of Kirton, and is also a well-known bowler; a local and county player, and former national president of the English Bowling Federation.

*"The Last Ditch," by David Lampe (Cassell 36s.).

Fred Fossitt's son, Jim Fossitt, supplied this article as it appeared in the Boston Standard Newspaper.

Mr. GEOFF HADFIELD, BEM., 97 years of age of Alford, Lincs, generously provided the following information.

THE ROYAL OBSERVER CORPS
No. 11 Group, Lincoln

The Chief Constable of Lincoln City Police started recruiting volunteers in 1936, they were sworn in by the police as Special Constables, and formed what became known as the Observer Corps. Their task was to identify and plot aircraft and in so doing became the 'Eyes and Ears' of the Royal Air Force. Sergeant E Taylor (later to become Inspector) was the driving force in recruiting and arranging regular weekly training sessions.

The Corps was mobilised in August 1939 and control was passed from the police to the Air Ministry. Then in 1941 the Corps received Royal status and from then on was known as the Royal Observer Corps. In 1942 they were given the RAF blue battle dress that they adopted as their working uniform, and were issued with tin hats and gas masks.

There were forty-three posts established in Lincolnshire, but there were extreme difficulties in the early days with instruments standing out in the open, exposed to the elements. Mainly the personnel themselves resolved the problem building shelters with sandbags and other material.

The Posts adopted a code name, for example in Lincolnshire the Alford Post on the Willoughby Road where Geoff carried out his duties, was 'How Three'. Fosdyke, south of where I live, was 'Dog Three' and Holbeach was 'Dog Two', my home town of Boston was 'Easy One'. Each Post has intriguing stories, and a detailed account can be found in S. Finn's book: **'Lincolnshire Air War 1939 - 1945'**, published in 1973.

In May 1944 - 796 men from the Royal Observer Corps were dispatched to various locations to assist in the preparation for the D-Day operation. Geoff Hadfield was posted to Bournemouth Training Depot and assumed the roll of Seaborne Observer with the rank of Petty Officer

Aircraft Identifier. Geoff, with a comrade was assigned to a US Navy troop ship, the SS Marine Raven, operating under the code name of 'Operation Neptune'. The SS Marine Raven sailed from Swansea Bay with the 2nd American Infantry Division on board, arriving at Omaha Beach on D-Day plus 2. The ship then sailed to Belfast in Ireland and took on board the 8th American Infantry Division that landed at Utah Beach on the 27th July 1944.

Geoff described living on board ship with the US Navy as hosts, as a life of luxury, nothing was spared to make them comfortable. The Americans were unable to identify enemy aircraft, and so they appreciated the presence of the two ROC's. Geoff was nine weeks away from home on this vital mission, yet another small cog in a mighty wheel that defeated the Hitler regime.

The Royal Observer Corps was 'stood down' on Saturday 12th August 1945 and re-established in 1947. In 1953 the ROC was re-grouped and the Alford Post moved to Ulceby Cross, in what became No. 15 Group, and the new underground Post was built in 1960.

Geoff Hadfield at the age of 32 years, joined the Observer Corps when it was first established in 1936, and was still a member when it 'closed down' in 1991. During his fifty-five years of unstinting service, Geoff was awarded the BEM in 1975 and has the rare honour of having two clasps to his ROC Medal. Surely a fitting tribute to a long serving and dedicated member of the Royal Observer Corps.

Stanley Naylor, 2001

THE ISLAND AT WAR

This story is compiled from the above book which are 'Memories of War-Time Life on the Isle of Dogs, East London', edited by Eve Hostettler.

Evacuation

Preparations for the evacuation of school age children from London (and other major cities) were made in advance of the outbreak of war. Children had to write out their evacuation instructions, and some schools rehearsed the procedure of departure with gas masks and sandwiches at the ready, several times before they actually set off. When the time came, partings were tearful: children did not know where they were going and parents had no idea when they would see their little ones again.

The official evacuation began on September 1st; it had been planned to move three and a half million school age children and pregnant mums, but in the end less than one and a half million moved. Most of them reached a place of safety by nightfall on 3rd September. A large number of people, estimated at two million or more, organised their own evacuation. When the threatened Blitz failed to materialise, many parents fetched their children home again, so that by January 1940, about half the official evacuees were back with their own families. When the Blitz began in September 1940, there was a second wave of evacuation. As the memories of Islanders show, there was a good deal of coming and going and for some the move away from the Island was a permanent one.

For many evacuees, the experience was painful and with hindsight it is clear that the authorities had put more effort into organising transport and the distribution of gas masks, and less into establishing whether host families were really suitable or not.

The First Days of the Blitz

After a year of suspense, the expected bombing raids finally began over East London in September 1940. In the first night, thousands of homes were destroyed, 430 civilians were killed and 1,600 seriously injured. All the preparations for fire-fighting, rescue work and first aid, so long rehearsed, were set in motion. But nothing had prepared people for the frightening intensity of the bombing. Some people had left the Island during the first year of the war; with the onset of the Blitz, many more left as quickly as they could, taking what little they could carry and fleeing the inferno which had been their home.

One of the Island landmarks which was destroyed in the first night of the raids was St Cuthbert's Church, in West Ferry Road.

Taking Shelter

Before the Blitz began, Anderson shelters, made of corrugated iron, were distributed to those households, which had space in yard or garden to accomodate them. Additionally, the basements of certain large buildings were designated public shelters and people also sought their own places of safety, one of these was the crypt under Christ Church and another was under the railway arches of the viaduct crossing Millwall Park. People used the shelters to varying degrees. Some automatically went into their Andy or nearest public shelter, night after night, others waited until they heard the sirens, others scorned the idea and slept in their own beds or in make-shift beds under the kitchen table. The large shelters fostered their own subculture too, when fears and discomforts were overcome by a sense of shared peril, a waving of the usual social bounders and the camaraderie of the nightly sing-song. However, after a number of accidents in the large shelters, a Home Office report in February 1942 said that among people in Poplar and on the Island there was: "a growing distrust of public shelters and a move towards Anderson's".

The Raids

From 7th September 1940, the raids on London *(covering the centre and West End as well as the East End)* continued for 76 consecutive nights, with one break on November 2nd when bad weather prevented flight. There were also raids during the hours of daylight. The raids continued during the spring and early summer of 1941. It is this nine month period which constituted the real 'Blitz' though the raids and the threat of raids continued with varying intensity for the duration of the war. After the initial terrifying shock, Islanders feared to live with the sudden warnings, the hurried scramble to get into the shelters or other place of safety, the wait until the 'All Clear'. Amongst memories of this bizarre routine many moments of horror and of fateful chance are vividly recalled.

War Work

Under war-time schemes for the mobilisation of labour, many Islanders, both men and women *(particularly in the case of the latter, those without family responsibilities)* were ordered to leave home and move to another part of the country to do work connected with the war effort. Women were engaged in munitions work and men often worked with boats and cargoes in other dockyard areas. Some managed to go with friends or other family members. As with the evacuees, the temporary move became a permanent one in some cases.

Everyday life

Nothing was normal and nothing was as it had been before. People were living out of suitcases and in all sorts of odd places - churches, schools, other people's homes, they had to change their jobs because their workplace was burned down, or because they were ordered to as part of the war effort, clothing, food and other necessities were in short supply and water, gas and electricity were often turned off. Emergency and voluntary services were hard-pressed to meet the needs of the temporarily homeless for food and warmth. Families were broken up and sometimes it was hard to keep in touch. Official arrangements for dealing with the misfortunes of war often lagged behind the events; the young and adventurous were able to cope, even to enjoy the challenge of the world turned upside down, but for the sick, elderly and disabled it was a bewildering and nerve-racking experience.

The Landscape of War

The overall impression from records made at the time from what was remembered years later, is of people struggling to behave normally in a world where houses, shops and factories had collapsed in heaps of burning rubble, a world of fire, of dust, of falling debris and black stinking smoke; and when this had cleared away, a world of desolation, where once-familiar streets were scarcely recognisable and neighbours and kin had vanished without trace. In September 1940 an official observer wrote: "The Isle of Dogs is like a district of the dead and nearly everyone who can go has gone". In 1945 in Cubitt Town, 75% of homes were found to be unfit for habitation. The population of the Island had shrunk from 21,000 to 9,000. One third of all warehousing was destroyed, as were many public buildings, including the Island Baths, Millwall Central School and twelve public houses.

Coming Home

For Islanders with relatives in the Armed Forces, news from the Front was always anxiously awaited. Home-comings were fraught with emotion and were often followed by a long-drawn out period of adjustment. Those returning on leave to the devastated Island were impressed by the suffering and the comparative helplessness of the unarmed civilian community. Some were unlucky enough to find their homes demolished and their families' dead or scattered.

The Auxiliary Services

As part of the war effort, many people of all ages were not called-up or otherwise engaged on essential work, volunteered for the auxiliary services. In places where bombing was expected to be severe, such as the Isle of Dogs, units of personnel were established and housed in existing public service buildings, taken over and equipped for war-time purposes. Schools were the most likely candidates for this, as it was expected that most children would be evacuated anyway. Existing fire, ambulance and police stations were also converted for the emergency. By 1943 the Island had three damage control centres, two ambulance stations, three civilian supply depots, two first-aid posts, five fire stations, a mobile canteen, a mortuary, three rescue centres, five rest stations and six air-raid warden posts.

As bombing raids did not start until a year after war was declared, there was plenty of time for training. Then suddenly on September 7th 1940 'the noise of battle was upon us' as Warden David Marson wrote in his diary. Walls collapsed in clouds of dust, warehouses burst into flames, giving off black smoke and poisonous fumes from the quantities of oils, chemicals, paints, minerals and raw materials of manufacture stored by Island firms. People were buried under the rubble or blown apart by the blast; some wandered about in a state of shock. Amid these scenes of chaos and destruction, which continued day and night for a period of several months, the auxiliary services were called on to put out fires, rescue the wounded, collect the dead and safeguard the living from unexploded bombs and damaged buildings. They were often in deadly peril, almost always dirty, hungry and short of sleep, glad of a drink and a laugh whenever they had the chance.

Extracts from David Marson's Diary 1940

Friday October 11th: There were 10 bombs dropped in St. Leonard's Road last night and I hear this morning that several were dropped on the GWR (Great Western Railway) at Ealing . . . we have had the usual visitation during the day. There goes the 'moaner' 7.15pm.

Saturday October 12th: We have had several raids this morning and fights in the air galore . . . the raids continued through the afternoon until 5 o'clock and so to tea and wait until the next wave. 7.15pm they're here again so I'm out once more.

Sunday October 13th: We had the monotonous drone of the unwelcome visitors again and the fireworks. The whiz bombs dropping and the happier, for us, music of our shells ploughing their way up to drive the hun further afield.

Monday October 14th: We had a proper Blitz from a quarter to seven till past twelve and the bombs and shells playing cross over almost unceasingly. We have had three alerts today but I have not heard of any damage done yet.

Tuesday October 15th: We have a very hot night with the guns and bombs causing the greatest noise since we had the great straffes of September 6, 7 and 8.

Wednesday October 16th: The night was one long blast even more terrible than the previous one. The marvellous thing is not that the bombs missed us but that there was again no panic and not much fear shown. We have had several warnings during the day, the worst being round about 5 o'clock when Glenmarmock Avenue was hit, there were several casualties some serious but no fatal ones up to now.

Friday October 18th: Last night (Thursday) was the fiercest we have had at this spot. The huns are being whacked and I suppose that this is one of their last kicks before they admit it.

Saturday October 19th: I was going to get a snack when the moaners got busy and when near home the overhead clients let go two bombs as a reminder that this is still the Isle of Dogs and the dock area. When I went into the house early this morning I found that the kitchen ceiling was reclining on the mat in front of the fire with a few air holes in the slates. I fortunately was able to carry most of it into the garden on the mats and rugs. What a mess! What a war!

Sunday October 20th: The Blitz seemed fiercer than ever last night and although no bombs dropped actually near, we were interested in a new idea. They tried out an incendiary which came down with a great rushing sound accompanied with enormous golden light which lit the place for miles like daylight and they caused several fires. Now we have seen them, we know them and will accept them as part of the nightly fare.

*The book '***The Island At War****' from which the above few pages have been extracted and printed with the kind permission of the Island History Trust, contains some thirty personal stories and more dates from David Marson's Diary. I am informed that unfortunately the book is out of print.*

WOMEN'S INSTITUTES (WI)

The WI thrived in hamlets and villages throughout the 1920's and 30's so that by 1938 the number of institutes had risen to 5,500 and membership was more than 350,000.

When World War II was declared on 3rd September 1939, the WI was in a prime position to assist the farming industry with poultry, dairy products and the potato harvest, for example. Then Lady Denham, Chairman of the WI National Executive Committee, was handed responsibility for the Women's Land Army. Both organisations were closely involved with food production, many of the WI members living in the country were already involved in farming, hence the close contact of the WI and WLA. 'Digging for Victory' was a widely used slogan that must have given some impetus to the food production in the British Isles.

During the war years the WI Movement distributed 140,000 fruit trees and 134,000 packets of seed that alone was a remarkable operation. But they were also able to get extra sugar to make jam from surplus fruit supplied by members, provided the jam was made on the premises of the local WI. Canning machines - quite a new thing for the British - could be obtained through the Ministry of Agriculture and the cans came from the Metal Box Company, enabling the WI to can fruit and tomatoes. Later on vegetables were included, but this was not such an easy operation as the fruit.

It was not until I came to research the activities of the WI during the war years on the 'Home Front', that I became aware of this massive operation. A small number of members in a hamlet may have only produced a few cans of fruit and a few jars of jam, but multiply that by 2,600 centres in 1940 and 4,500 in 1941 and production must have been enormous.

Knitting is associated with our women and many of them used their skills to produce woollen goods for all the Forces. Perhaps this is a good time to express my thanks and appreciation for parcels that I received.

Especially for one that arrived in the Shetlands from the Kirton 'Comforts Fund' in the winter of 1943, containing a rolled neck pullover, scarf, long white woollen stockings - useful with the wellies that were worn almost daily - and gloves. No doubt the WI would have been involved who organised knitting parties that produced countless articles all welcomed by everyone, whether in the Navy, Army or Air Force.

The WI was also involved with the evacuees and no doubt many other activities not mentioned.

Trying to learn more about the WI during the war years, I had a very interesting talk to Hilda Hall, who is a very sprightly eighty-five years of age and an active member of Frampton WI. Hilda informed me that the ordinary subscription in mid 1930's was 2/6 - 2s 6d - but a further payment of 4s 0d, making a total of 6s 6d, ($32^1/_2$p in today's currency) entitled her to all facilities available to a full member.

Not only was Hilda involved in the WI in the hamlet of Algarkirk near Boston, but she was also a member of the WVS; ARP; Forces Comforts Fund; and was a member of St. John's Ambulance Association for the duration of the war. During the summer months, she worked on a farm helping with the 'Dig for Victory' campaign. Hilda must, therefore, be a shining example of thousands of women on the 'Home Front' all over the country, which helped in the Victory over Europe.

Mr Churchill said at a special meeting of the WI at Nottingham in 1943, that 'the enemy hoped we would grow weary but no community in the world was better organised than ours. We were ready for any form of air attack, ready to grow more food, make more munitions and more ships, care for the sick and wounded and maintain civilian life. This would not be possible but for the women'.

I first became aware of the WI - as mentioned in my story on weekend leave - when I made good use of a bike the Kirton WI stored at Boston Police Station for the use of all serving personnel. I'm not sure how the female species would have coped, even though I am aware how resourceful they are, because it was a male model!

Then in 1981, during my coach-driving career, I conveyed a party from the Cowbridge WI to Denham College near Abingdon. As all WI members are aware, the college is set in a beautiful park in Berkshire and is the seat of learning where a range of subjects are taught.

There are two books that illustrate the WI: 'Live and Learn', the story of Denham College 1948 - 1969 by Barbara Kaye and 'Village Voices' A Portrait of Change in England's Green and Pleasant Land 1915 - 1990 by Piers Dudgeon. I acknowledge that both books have helped me to compile this story with the guidance of Hilda Hall.

Stanley Naylor

"We shall fight on the seas and oceans, we shall fight with growing confidence and growing strength in the air, we shall defend our island, whatever the cost may be. We shall fight on the beaches, we shall fight on the landing grounds, we shall fight in the fields and in the streets, we shall fight in the hills, we shall never surrender".

Winston Churchill, June 1940

A KNITTING LYRIC

Around in little groups we sit,
    Our needles clicking as we knit.
Warm scarves and socks and helmets, too,
    In kharki shades and Air Force blue.

Mittens and gloves we also make;
    Knit one, purl one and then intake;
They'll bring some warmth to those so brave
    Who've gone to fight and England save.

And operation socks are made
    Ready for those who need their aid.
Who're wounded in the battle fight -
    We'll help them too, with all our might.

In ev'ry home throughout the land,
    The women all they take a hand,
At making something warm to knit,
    For all who've gone to do their bit.

So as we knit and purl one, too,
    We think of all those brave and true;
Their courage may it stand the test.
    And may God's blessing on them rest.

(Unknown author) Boston Guardian, May 1940
By permission of The British Library

THE ROYAL AIR FORCE

I am aware of the tremendous task undertaken by both the Royal Navy and Merchant Shipping, and their tremendous losses for which we all remember with sadness. The Army was vigilantly defending our shores, plus their activities in various parts of the country meant that soldiers were an integral part of local communities.

However, in September 1940, in the height of the Battle of Britain, often referred to as the turning point of the Second World War, Winston Churchill stated to his Cabinet colleagues that it would be a long time before the Army could return to the Continent. The Navy's traditional weapon of blockade had been 'blunted' by the enemy, only bombing therefore by the Royal Air Force (RAF) in the foreseeable future could seriously injure Germany.

From 1939 to 1945 the RAF was indeed a part of the 'Home Front', having establishments all over the UK, many of them in the counties bordering the East and South coasts. Thus the RAF blue uniforms mingling with the khaki of the Army and the dark blue of the Navy, became a familiar sight in our villages, towns and cities.

Huge construction work took place building aerodromes that had a bigger population than some villages, in fact they became the 'life blood' of the community in which they were built.

These are the numbers of personnel - including WAAF'S on 'dromes in the UK on which I was stationed, 1941 to 1944:

RAF Tangmere, Sussex. Opened 1918. Personnel 4,398.

RAF Sumburgh, Shetland Isles. Opened 1936. Personnel 1,321. No WAAFS.

RAF Wick, Scotland. Opened 1939. Personnel 3,606.

RAF Predannack, Cornwall. Opened 1941. Personnel 2,153.

RAF Blakehill Farm, Wiltshire. Opened 1944. Personnel 2,701.

RAF Middle Wallop, Hampshire. Opened 1940. Personnel 2,252.

RAF North Weald, Essex. Opened 1940. Personnel 3,860.

With all the RAF auxiliary units in Lincolnshire, including hospitals, radio stations, bombing ranges, plus the forty-five aerodromes, it can be seen there was a considerable high number of RAF personnel in this part of the Home Front in what was known as 'Bomber County'. I am therefore going to take RAF East Kirkby as an example of a bomber station.

There were three phases to the now closed RAF Station, East Kirkby. The first phase was the construction of a 'Dummy' or 'Decoy' site at Back Lane, Hagnaby, on the East side of the 'drome. It was in 1940 that the Air Ministry decided that decoy airfields were constructed in an effort to divert enemy bombers from the main airfields. Hagnaby in Lincolnshire being some twelve miles from Boston and five miles from Spilsby, was ideal being between the sea and RAF Station Coningsby.

Mr Huby Fairhead, Secretary of the Norfolk and Suffolk Aviation Museum, informs me that Hagnaby was a KQ site. 'K' being a 'Day decoy airfield' and 'Q' being a 'Night - Lightning - decoy airfield'.

Reference information in the book 'Fields of Deception' by Colin Dobinson, published by Methuen 2000, P49 states that Hagnaby KQ site opened around mid-March 1940 and P126 states the site closed between the last week in June and the first week in July 1941.

The second phase followed the closure of the 'Decoy' site at Hagnaby. Work soon began constructing the new airfield between the 'Decoy' site and the village of East Kirkby which subsequently became RAF Station, East Kirkby. When construction of the airfield was completed, the famous Lancaster bomber aircraft soon established itself on the station, as did personnel that totalled some 2,400.

I have great admiration for aircrews of bomber aircraft that night after night endured hazardous raids over Germany. I am sure, however, they would be the first to admit their missions could not have been completed without the help of dedicated ground crews and ancillary workers who tend not to get the recognition they deserve.

As already mentioned, an aerodrome such as East Kirkby was like a small town and would be a typical example of most aerodromes, that I knew anyway. This is a brief description of what constituted an Aerodrome.

Most of the aircraft stood out in the open at dispersal points around the perimeter where men worked in all weathers to prepare the planes for the next trip. There were huge hangers that were used mainly for major repairs. Other buildings included the Control Tower - we referred to it as the Watch Tower; Head Quarters was the hub of the station; Sick Quarters - including the dreaded dentist; Officers, SNCO's and Airmen/WAAF's messes. Yes there were WAAF's on most stations, unfortunately none at Sumburgh, but around 480 were resident at East Kirkby. They had separate sleeping quarters, even though they mixed with their male comrades for meals in the mess according to their rank.

The MT Section provided vehicles for every eventuality, plus there would be fuel storage both for the vehicles and aircraft, different octane, of course. We did have one incident in Germany when Jerry cans got mixed and we used aviation fuel in the vehicles. The high octane certainly made a Ford V8 engine in a 15 cwt truck run very sweetly, but we had to dilute it with ordinary fuel before it caused trouble with the valves.

Returning to buildings on an Aerodrome, the NAAFI was the most popular - although on some stations the Church Army provided an excellent service. Then there was the clothing store, barber shop, gymnasium, cinema, church, bomb dump, fire station, sewage works. Finally the Guardroom with the SP's and the RAF Regiment ensuring security of a close knit community.

I don't intend to delve into the history of RAF Station, East Kirkby, Geoff D Copeman in his book **'SILKSHEEN'** has covered this adequately.

The third phase that has emerged on the site of the closed RAF Station at East Kirkby, is the **'Lincolnshire Aviation Heritage Centre'**. Exhibits include the centre piece, a Lancaster bomber - the 'City of Sheffield' or 'Just Jane'. This Lancaster is beautifully preserved with four functional Merlin engines that enables the aircraft to taxi up and down the runway on special days, but is not permitted to fly at the time of writing.

Other exhibits include a Bedford 'Queen Mary', BSA Dispatch Motor Bike; Jeep; Fordson Crew Bus and a Foam Tender and David Brown Tug Tractor. There is a fully restored Control Tower, Chapel, Fire Station and the NAAFI. Lincolnshire Aircraft Recovery Group has a fine display of aircraft parts they have recovered from crashed aircraft. All this is displayed in a Pictorial History and Guide book just printed and is available from the centre.

Stanley Naylor

* inky pinky parley voo !

As in their modern battle rig they tramp along, the boys sing the same old ditties.

They still plead with Daisy, Daisy to give them her answer do; still keep the home fire burning; still court the fickle mademoiselle from Armentières. Somehow the newer songs cannot quite capture the lilt, the gaiety, the gusto of Tipperary.

Why, ask yourself, should this be? Why out of thousands of songs that since have come and gone, why should these old favourites remain favourites? Why?

Because their goodness, their quality, their aptness, was such as never to be forgotten. The voices of a million marching men *advertised* the greatness of these simple tunes; of these immortal songs.

And as with great songs, so with great products. *Advertising* has proclaimed the qualities behind a host of famous names. Such names and such qualities cannot be forgotten.

IF A THING'S BRANDED AND CONSISTENTLY ADVERTISED IT'S BOUND TO BE GOOD.

Issued by the Advertising Association.

Boston Guardian, September 1941

STAND THOSE THREE TOWERS?

Stand those three towers still a-pointing
In the dawn light, stark and clear?
Does the ghostly roar of the 'Lanc' still soar
O'er the fields of Lincolnshire?

Do the shades of Ancient Briton;
Of Roman, Saxon, Dane;
Still stand and gaze in mute amaze
On the ghosts who throng the plain?

Ghosts of the flower of England;
Of Empire and Allied Kin;
Are they still in sight in the darkening light
Each dusk as the night rolls in?

Ghosts of Geordie, Scouse and Cockney,
Of Yellowbelly and Tyke;
Do they fly again over Martin Fen;
O'er Grimsby and Boston Dyke?

And of Paddy, Jock and Taffy;
Of Aussie, Canuck and Yank.
Are they flying still over Lindum Hill,
O'er the Wash and the Humber Bank?

And the Freedom Men of Europe;
New Zealand and Afric' dark;
Do they still fly strong to the Merlin's song
And the sound of the Browning's bark?

Do those hosts of glad young warriors
Still soar and fly and toil
And fight and die in an alien sky;
Still rest in an alien soil?

Ah! Many the distant lonely cross
And many the shattered 'plane
Whose last home sight on a bombers' night
Was a view of a Lincoln Lane.

Does the lumbering bus still rumble
Those lanes from -thorpe to -by?
Does it still stop hard by the old churchyard
Where more of our brothers lie?

Sons of all the warring nations;
The plain men and the brave.
All troubles past; they've found their last
Safe home in an English grave.

While we, whom they've left behind them;
We few, as our years grow old
Still fight and fly in their battle sky
In dreams when the night is cold.

Ah! Lincoln! Our shire of memories
From the dawn to the setting sun;
Your heath and fen will live again
With us till our journey's run.

© *Victor Cavendish*

A BRIEF HISTORY OF AIR SEA RESCUE OPERATIONS FROM LINCOLNSHIRE 1939 - 1945

Location of Lincolnshire Air Sea Rescue Bases 1939 - 1945

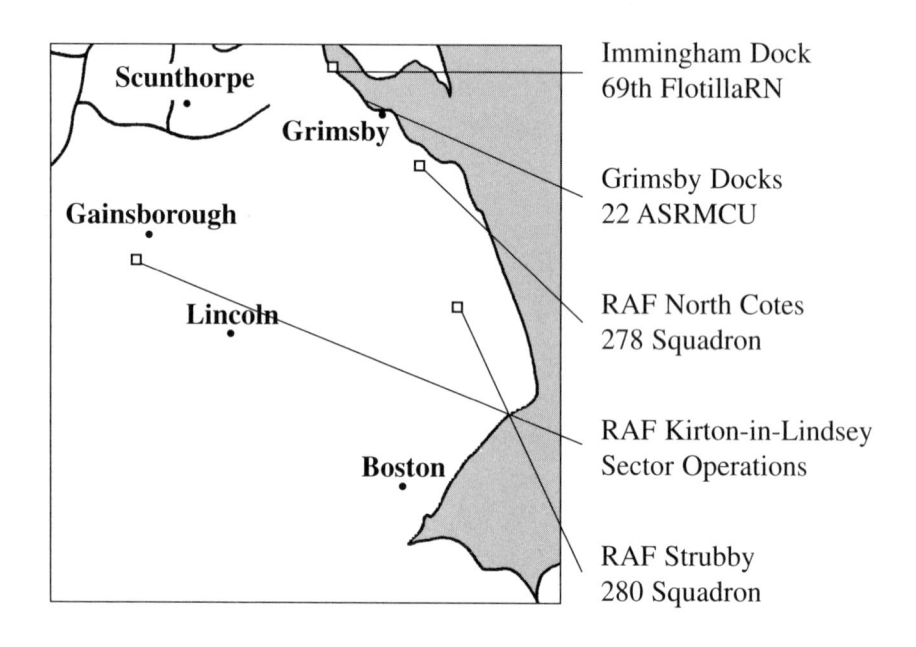

Immingham Dock
69th FlotillaRN

Grimsby Docks
22 ASRMCU

RAF North Cotes
278 Squadron

RAF Kirton-in-Lindsey
Sector Operations

RAF Strubby
280 Squadron

Royal Air Force Air Sea Rescue Operations:

Air Sea Rescue Developments Prior to 1941

The question of safety arrangements of aircrews over flying the North Sea was first raised by the Air Officer Commanding (AOC) Bomber Command, Air Chief Marshall Sir E R Ludlow Hewitt, at a conference in December 1938. Concern was expressed that planned air strikes against an occupied Europe could be severely curtailed through the lack of rescue facilities.

Air sea rescue operations up to this time had been dependant upon the co-operation of several agencies. The search for a downed aircraft at that time involving: - the squadron from which the aircraft concerned was attached: the diversion of Naval or merchant vessels in the area (via GPO Wireless Transmitter [W/T] stations); and the use of civil aerodromes W/T and public telephones to contact lifeboat stations and the coastguard.

To extend these facilities 8 High Speed Launches (HSL's) were stationed around Britain at Manston, Felixstowe, Donibristle (Fife), Tayport, Pembroke Dock and Calshot (2). Although this was an improvement it still left a stretch of coast between Felixstowe and Tayport without cover, and this resulted in a further 13 HSL's being deployed during 1939 - one being allocated to Grimsby. [1]

Although it is clear that the authorities had made every effort to introduce a sound system, the first few months of hostilities highlighted that the peacetime rescue organisations would not function effectively in wartime. Extensive delays were experienced with the public telephone system, which in turn affected communication with the RNLI and HM Coastguard. Broadcasts to shipping were halted to prevent information being of use to the enemy and the dispersal of aircraft against attack both affected response times. It also became evident that many of the 220 air crew reported killed or missing during July 1940 had last been seen over the sea and this led to speculation by senior officers as to how many of these air crew had survived attacks only to come down in the sea to die of exposure. [2]

Attempts were made to improve this state of affairs including an ad hoc arrangement between the Air Officer Commanding 11 Group Fighter Command (AVM Keith Park) and Vice Admiral, Dover (Sir Bertram H. Ramsey) which provided a local rescue service using light naval craft to supplement HSL's and Westland Lysanders as spotter aircraft.

Further meetings were held throughout 1940 and 1941 and these ultimately resulted with executive control of RAF air sea rescue being transferred to RAF Coastal Command from RAF Fighter Command with effect from 1st February 1941. Further to this a multi service committee meeting held on the 14th January 1941 determined that a new Air Sea Rescue Directorate would take over full responsibility for operations. [3]

Grimsby Docks: 22 Royal Air Force High Speed launch Unit

As the 'Phoney War' (as the first months of the war became to be known) gave way to the Battle of Britain and intensified hostilities, so did the need for rescue facilities to cover the vast expanse of the North Sea.

RAF Bomber Command was beginning to mould itself into the efficient war machine that it was to become by mid 1944, and RAF Coastal Command was intensifying its raids of the coastline of Occupied Europe, indeed activity continued to increase locally at RAF North Coates (with it's Coastal Command squadrons of anti-shipping Beauforts and Hudsons) and at the increasing number of Bomber Command airfields that were impressing themselves on the Lincolnshire landscape.

The increased activity along with increased resources available to the Air Sea Rescue Directorate resulted in the arrival of 22 High Speed Launch Unit at Grimsby in June 1940. What actually transpired between 1939 and 1941 is difficult to determine from official records since contemporary records have yet to be found, however, there is evidence to support the case that a HSL was stationed in Grimsby Docks and did provide rescue facilities both in the North Sea and during the

Dunkirk evacuation.

A geographical index of Home units as at 30th December 1942, gives the postal address of 22 High Speed Launch unit as, "Royal Docks, Grimsby, Lincolnshire. Telephone GY 3856". Transport facilities were at Grimsby Docks LNER, ½ mile (passenger & goods). The Local Movement Control Office was at York and the Area HQ for Works Staff was No. 2 at Retford. [6]

As facilities were expanded at Grimsby so did the need for support requirements for the crews. Spencer Capper served as a Medic from early 1942 until 1944 and recalls that shortly before his arrival the unit had requisitioned two large houses in Abbey Road (No's. 22 and 24). Prior to this the crews had been billeted in either "The Flying Angel" or the "Mission to Deep Sea Fishermen".

The accommodation in Abbey Road was used by all NCO's and Other Ranks, unless they had Sleeping Out Passes (SOP's) or lived locally. The downstairs of one house was used as the Mess with the cookhouse at the rear, an RAF Sergeant Cook being in charge. The front room of the other house was used as a recreation area with tables, chairs, books and a record player. Initially the crews themselves were responsible for keeping the house clean and tidy but operational requirements soon necessitated the employment of two ladies to do these chores. Although each house had a bathroom, there was only cold water so the crews either used hot showers in the HQ building down at the Dock Basin, or used the local public baths in Orwell Street. Recreational facilities were provided by various denominations of churches as well as cinemas and dance halls such as the Cafe Dansant at Cleethorpes.

Spencer particularly remembers the morale boosting efforts of the various organisations, and especially the School of Art in Silver Street. Here, Spencer was taught woodcarving by a Mr Robson. He also remembers the kindness and hospitality shown by Mr Robson and the other older students to a certain 18 year old who was away from home for the first time. 22 ASRMCU were also extended the facilities of the Ticklers Sports Club free of charge. Numerous dances were organised by the hospitals with crew members always invited. Spencer was impressed by the hospitality and friendship of the families living around Abbey Road. Many crew struck up friendships of varying depths, particularly with the young ladies at the Abbey Laundry. An additional benefit of the latter was the extra special starching of shirt collars. Initially crews used public transport to get down to the Docks but later on were issued with RAF bicycles.

As at April 1943 the unit, which had now been renamed 22 Air Sea Rescue Marine Craft Unit, had the following complement:- [7]

Marine Craft:	4 + 1 High Speed Launches
Marine Craft Crews:	5 Officers
	10 Senior NCO's
	43 Other Ranks
Base Party:	1 Senior NCO
	5 Other Ranks

Equipment

The Unit operated a number of high speed launch types, with the two most common being the Type Two 63ft "Whaleback" and the Type Three 68ft "Hants & Dorset".

Type Two 63' High Speed Launch "Whaleback"

The "Whaleback" was built by the British Power Boat Company (BPBC), between 1940 and 1942. The launch was 63ft long, with a beam of 16^1/$_2$ ft and a draught of 3ft 10 inches and had been adapted from an existing design for a Motor Anti-Submarine Boat. The Whaleback nickname was given by the crews who were impressed by the types racy lines and high speed. [8]

Powered by three 500hp Power Napier Sea Lion petrol engines, the

Whaleback had a top speed of 35 knots (for $\frac{1}{2}$ hour), or 28 knots (continuous). Its range was 420 nautical miles. [9]

Following attacks on HSL's, the initial armament of one or two light machine guns was increased to a pair of twin gun turrets and a 20mm Oerlikon cannon.

Of the 69 boats built the following Whalebacks operated at sometime during their service life from Grimsby:

No's. 124; 125; 130; 131; 139; 141; 142; 144; 157; and 188 [10]

Type Three High Speed Launch "Hants and Dorset"

The "Hants & Dorset" was another BPBC design, which was aimed at overcoming the shortcomings of the Whaleback, namely better accommodation and increased range. The Type Three acquired its nickname from the likeness of its awkward top-heavy appearance to the South Coast Bus Company's double decker buses.

The "Hants & Dorset" was 68ft in length, had a beam of 17ft and a draught of 4ft 3ins. Powered by three 500hp Power Napier Sea Lion petrol engines, the launch had a maximum speed of $28\frac{1}{2}$ knots (for $\frac{1}{2}$ hr) and $23\frac{1}{2}$ knots (continuous). Its range was 580 nautical miles. [11]

Of the 89 boats built mostly during 1943, the following operated from Grimsby sometime during their service life:

No's. 2559; 2560; 2572; 2573; 2574; 2576; 2578; 2579; 2594; 2612; 2664; 2677; 2678. [12]

Operations and crew recollections

Mr Wally Bramhall of Hull was posted to 22 High Speed Launch Unit following leave after three years service in Aden and a Coxswains course at Calshot. Wally's first three months were spent as NCO responsible for bicycles! Wally's "real" work started when he became Second Coxswain on HSL 131.

Wally recalls seeing HSL 111 beached on the mud bank in the Dock Basin - her back broken following an encounter with an acoustic mine during a high-speed test run. The incident had a silver lining in that it provided a ferry crew to deliver Canadian built launches which had arrived at Avonmouth Docks, Bristol in August 1941. The ferry crew had been formed in June 1941 under Flt. Lt. Bowen of 22 HSL Unit, were HSL 139 and HSL 141 were u/s and allocated for use for spares. The crew provided by HSL 111's demise left for Ramsgate on June 24th to pick up HSL 121 which was destined for Calshot and shipping overseas. This task carried out, the crew returned to Grimsby and ferried HSL 141 to Newport. [13]

Mr F Hanson of Bradford was stationed at Grimsby from late 1942 to early 1943 and remembers HSL 131 colliding with a tug, the "Flying Dutchman", in the entrance to the outer harbour. '131' came off worse, losing it's bows from a point just behind the starboard side to a point forward of the wheel house on the port side. The HSL was towed to a slipway for repairs, which were carried out by Base personnel. (HSL 131 went on to serve at Acklington, Tayport, Littlehampton, and Felixstowe before being sunk off the mouth of the Thames Estuary by two Focke Wulf 190's). [14]

Mr Frank Shelton, of Grimsby was posted to 22 ASRMCU for five months during the latter part of 1943, on attachment from 16 Group HQ Frank served as Second Wireless Operator on HSL 2560, one of five "Hants & Dorset" type launches based at Grimsby at that time. Frank was a crew member when '2560' achieved its first success in the late summer of 1943.

The rescue of 6 survivors from the crew of an Avro Lancaster is typical of the high degree of co-ordination in ASR. A Coastal Command Anson had spotted the Lancaster and '2560' had been scrambled. To help ensure success a second Anson and two Hudsons guided the HSL from Spurn Point to the dinghy, some hours away, 40 miles east of Skegness.

A second, somewhat lengthier, rescue illustrates the teamwork that existed between the various units. The rescue, made in 1941, involved an Armstrong Whitworth Whitley, which had been hit in both engines by fire from night fighters whilst returning from a raid on Berlin. The Whitley ditched 90 miles from the Humber Estuary in the early hours of the morning. The aircraft exploded shortly after the crew had paddled clear in their dinghy, which had overturned during the evacuation. The crew clung to the upturned dinghy for two days, being sighted on the first day by another Whitley (which lost sight of them due to high seas), and then by a Hudson on the following day, which dropped supplies and flame floats. Further assistance was given later on day two by a Hampden, which dropped Lindholme Gear. The crew were picked up before nightfall by a Grimsby based HSL. [15]

In May 1943 HSL 2579 accompanied by two Royal Naval RML's was involved with the first rescue utilising an Airborne Lifeboat. [16] On 5th May 1943 a Handley Page Halifax of 102 Squadron was hit by flak over Dortmund. The aircraft suffered the loss of two engines, crossing the Dutch coast at 8,000 ft and gradually losing height. The aircraft ditched fifty miles off Spurn Head with all the crew safely getting clear, despite having to release the dinghy manually. After three hours, at 06.25 hrs, an ASR Hudson was seen and Very lights were fired. The Hudson fixed the position of the dinghy as 53°40'N 01°26'E and after an hour a second Hudson was overhead carrying an Airborne Lifeboat. The second Hudson was also accompanied by a third Hudson.

The lifeboat was dropped and all mechanisms worked as designed. The crew familiarised themselves with the equipment and started the engine. The Hudson flew overhead and flashed by Aldis lamp a course to steer. Initially the crew towed their dinghy but a broken painter necessitated its sinking by gunfire from an escorting Hudson. Shortly before noon the escorting aircraft lost sight of the lifeboat due to low cloud and the lifeboat also developed engine trouble. The crew rigged a sail and at 13.00 hrs the lifeboat was spotted again by a Hudson. The launches were now given a new course to steer and following assistance from an Anson and a Walrus, HSL 2579 located the lifeboat, picked up the crew and returned to Grimsby. The lifeboat was taken in tow and moored to a channel buoy about 25 miles from Grimsby, were it was later recovered from by a Naval patrol boat. Although the initial reports stated that all equipment had functioned as designed, further research revealed that this was not the case. However, several of these failings were rectified immediately afterwards and many important lessons had been learned. July 1999 saw the 2 surviving aircrew and 1 of 3 surviving HSL crewman being guests of honour at a Civic Reception hosted by North East Lincolnshire Council.

Although the Unit operated out of the Royal Dock Basin whenever possible there were times when the weather conditions required the two Duty HSL's to sail for Immingham and moor close to the Royal Navy rescue launches based there. 22 ASRMCU was to continue its important work until 16th December 1945. The Unit was disbanded on the 8th August 1946. (17)

The Establishment and Strength return for the Unit as at the 16th December 1945 is detailed below:

22 ASRMCU Establishment as at 16th December 1945(18)

Rank	Establishment	Actual
Officers	4	3
Airmen	59	5
Airwomen	2	55
Civilians	2	0
Total	67	63

Rescues performed by local trawlers

Although it was not until August 1941 that HSL's of 22 Marine Craft Unit were recorded as being based at Grimsby Docks, there had been ad hoc facilities provided by the many trawlers that sailed from the port. One of the earlier reported successes was the rescue of the crew of a 9 Squadron Vickers Wellington (Serial No. N2983), on 18th December 1939.

The aircraft had earlier been detailed to carry out a reconnaissance and attack on the German Fleet at Wilhelmshaven. The Wellington, flown by Sergeant Ramshaw, suffered repeated and determined attacks by Messerschmitt Bf 110's of 1/ZG76 (Staffel 1 of Zerstorgruppe 76), with extensive damage being inflicted on the main fuel tanks, leaving 30 minutes flying time on reserve tanks.

The Wellington was forced to ditch at 50° 16'N 01° 15'E approximately 400 yards from the Grimsby trawler Erillus (GY 516), Ramshaw having spotted the vessel ahead of the aircraft as the engines died. The Erillus picked up 5 survivors, (the rear gunner already having been critically wounded was lost with the aircraft) and landed them at Grimsby. [4]

Immingham Dock and the 69th Flotilla Royal Navy Rescue Marine Launches

Although based primarily at Grimsby's Royal Dock Basin, there were times when the weather conditions required the two 22 ASRMCU Duty HSL's to sail for Immingham. Immingham was also the base for the Royal Navy's 69th Rescue Motor Launch (RML) flotilla. The Unit operated 4 Fairmile B launches. (HMRML 547 [Lead Ship] 520, 550 and 553 The Fairmiles were considerably slower than the HSL's but being larger were able to withstand bad weather better and had a greater endurance. The Fairmile B was 112 ft long, had a beam of 18$\frac{1}{4}$ ft and a draft of 4$\frac{3}{4}$ft. It's two Hall Scott 1200 hp Defender engines gave it a top speed of 20 knots and a cruising speed of 16$\frac{1}{2}$ knots. Whilst at Immingham the RMLs carried out numerous searches and between 21st May 1943 and 30th April 1944 were responsible for rescuing 48 men in 10 successful "crash calls". The Flotilla was reassigned to Dartmouth and left Immingham on 10th May 1944.

The port remained an alternate mooring for the Grimsby based HSL's until 22ASRMCU was disbanded, however, a strong post war link was maintained by the presence of 1110 Marine Craft Unit between September 1949 and February 1958. 1110 MCU was equipped with 3 launches (Hants & Dorset's 2740 and 2743 and Seaplane Tender 1510)

The Unit's role was to provide rescue cover both within Sea Area Humber and off the RAF Bombing Range at Donna Nook. A similar function was provided further down the Lincolnshire coast by 1109 MCU, which operated out of the Port of Boston between January 1956 and July 1958.

Airborne Air Sea Rescue operations

Whilst the HSL's formed the backbone of the RAF's rescue operations there was also considerable support provided by Air Sea Rescue Squadrons operating out of RAF North Coates, RAF Strubby and RAF Kirton in Lindsey.

RAF NORTH COATES

RAF North Coates first saw active service during the First World War, opening as a Night Landing Ground for 33 Squadron in 1916. During the inter war years it provided an armament training practice camp. Six months after the outbreak of hostilities the airfield was transferred to 16 Group Coastal Command and for the remainder of the war the Station's Beauforts, Swordfish, Hudsons and Beaufighters played a decisive role in anti-shipping strikes.

North Coates link with Air Sea Rescue is three fold. Firstly a detachment Flight of 278 ASR Squadron Westland Lysanders operated from the airfield between November 1941 and January 1943. Secondly, the base acted as the administrative Parent Unit for No. 22 High Speed Launch Unit (based at Grimsby Docks) and finally 275 Squadron provided a Westland Sycamore helicopter on detachment for search and rescue duties between February 1955 and October 1957.

The 278 Squadron detachment consisted of 3 aircraft of a type, which had originally been designed for Army co-operation duties. The aircraft had a very low stalling speed and was an ideal platform for search duties up to twenty miles offshore. The aircraft carried inflatable dinghies and emergency supplies in containers loaded onto wing spats. These supplies being dropped as closely to possible as the ditched aircrew. [5]

North Coates final role was to provide a key element of the defence of United Kingdom airspace with Bloodhound Surface to Air Guided Weapons (SAM's in modern day parlance). The Bloodhounds stayed from April 1957 until the airfields closure on 18th December 1986.

278 Air Sea Rescue Squadron

The Squadron's role was to assist ASR operations by patrolling the Lincolnshire and Yorkshire coasts and acting as spotter planes, locating ditched aircrew and dropping dinghies and supplies before directing 22 ASRMCU HSL's to the airmen. The Squadron's Lysander III's were powered by a single Bristol Mercury 30 radial engine, which gave a maximum speed of 190 mph. The aircraft had a range of 600 miles and the stub 'spat wings' carried Type M dinghies, smoke floats and food containers.

278's Operational Record Book contains many examples of the Unit's work, one example being detailed below:

24th July 1942   Lysander IIIA (Serial No. V9369)

Pilot: Flt/Sgt Telford Wireless Op/Air Gunner: Flt/Sgt Burdekin
Aircraft up: 06:15hrs   Aircraft down: 08:15hrs

Search completed successfully. Pilot found crew of Wellington aircraft (5 men) in dinghy about 6 miles off Mablethorpe almost immediately on arrival in search area. A fix was given to Kirton in Lindsey Operations, a smoke float and a dinghy were dropped. The aircraft then flew off to a Minesweeper or Trawler and signalled by Aldis lamp 'Men Down In Sea' but receiving no reply whatsoever the aircraft returned to dinghy (approx. 2 miles from vessel) and circled until the arrival of HSL 144 which rescued 5 men an hour later. A Wellington of 115 Squadron landed at North Coates in the afternoon and picked up the four uninjured crew. The Wellington involved in this rescue was a Mark III of 115 Squadron. The aircraft had taken off from RAF Marham to attack

Duisburg. Over the target the aircraft received major flak damage when a shell bursting directly beneath the aircraft stripped all of the fabric from the under surfaces. The pilot (Flt / Sgt E. Boutilier) successfully ditched the aircraft. Two crew members were slightly injured.

RAF STRUBBY

RAF Strubby operated 280 Squadron Vickers Warwick aircraft between May and September 1944. This twin-engine design evolved from the famous Vickers Wellington bomber and inherited the characteristic of being able to absorb heavy damage. The type was equipped with an air borne lifeboat and carried further rescue aids and supplies in the bomb bay. The good endurance of this aircraft made it suitable to conduct searches right up to the Dutch coast.

280 Squadron arrived from Thornaby under the command of Wing Commander McIntosh - better known to many at that time as 'All Weather Mac'. Mac's nickname had been earned for his outstanding flying abilities flying the fledgling commercial air services between London and Paris in the years immediately after the First World War. Flying converted bombers, Mac (and his contemporaries) flew in open cockpits in all weathers, using railway lines and other landmarks as their means of navigation.

The professionalism and expertise of the Squadron resulted in a high degree of coordination between launches and aircraft. Indeed, the search patterns used were refined to such a degree that the Squadron was able to implement standing patrols across the length and breadth of the North Sea, enabling the Warwicks to be on hand as soon as a stricken aircraft broadcast it's Mayday message. There are instances when Warwicks were so quick off the mark that they were on scene as aircraft were ditching, enabling the downed crews to board an airborne lifeboat within minutes of hitting the water.

RAF KIRTON-IN LINDSEY

RAF Kirton-in-Lindsey operated a number of Supermarine Spitfires in an ASR role, these being drawn from whichever squadrons were resident at the time and consisting of patrols over the North Sea for specific aircraft or as searches in general.

THE RECKONING

All told the Allied launches, destroyers, trawlers, etc saved over 13,000 lives between 1939 to 1945. Aircrew accounted for some 9,000 of these, nationality not an issue, nor which side rescue came from. The ASR service picked up anyone, regardless of nationality, the Germans did the same. Many thousands of hours were spent in the hostile, cold, dark waters of the North Sea, the Adriatic, The Mediterranean, the Atlantic and the Pacific. We will not know how many crews survived the ditching only to die from exposure, but what is apparent is the esteem that the 'webfoots' are held in by the aircrews. Only recently a Lincolnshire air-gunner, awarded the DFM for his efforts, spoke in glowing terms of the ASR crews, 'We knew you were down there in the darkness, waiting for our return, of course we knew the odds against finding a pin-prick of a dinghy in the vastness of an angry sea were stacked heavily against us, yet we knew you were there and that's what counted'.

Between May 1942 and December 1945 (official figures for May 1940 to April 1942 are sketchy) 22ASRMCU carried out 162 searches, expending some 1200 hours with and without success. 107 survivors (including 3 German) were picked up as well as 5 bodies. The figures speak for themselves, more than ample evidence to reiterate the ASR service's motto: *The sea shall not have them.*

Graham Richard Chaters, 2001

REFERENCES

1. Chartres, J. Fly for Their Lives (Airlife, 1988) pp 6

2. ibid pp 7

3. AIR 2 6257 ASR Organisation assorted papers
   (Public Records Office)

4. AIR 27 125 9 Squadron Operational Record Book [ORB] (PRO)

5. AIR 27 1605 278 Squadron ORB (PRO)

6. AIR 2 6257   ASR Organisation assorted papers
   (Public Records Office)

7. AIR 29 443 22 ASRMCU ORB (PRO)

8. Pereira, W. D., Boat in the Blue (Line One, 1985) pp 184 - 185

9. ibid. pp 183

10. ibid. pp 186 - 190

11. ibid. pp 196

12. ibid. pp 198 - 201

13. Pilborough, G. D., The History of RAF Marine Craft 1918 - 1886
    Vol. 2 (1839 - 1945) (Canimpex, 1987) pp 150

14. ibid.

15. Chartres, J. Fly for Their Lives (Airlife, 1988) pp 24 - 25

16. AIR 2 6257   ASR Organisation assorted papers
    (Public Records Office)

17. AIR 29 443 22 ASRMCU ORB (PRO)

18. ibid.

19. ibid.

BIBLIOGRAPHY

Books

Blackman, E., Airman at the Helm (Kenneth Mason, 1979)

Bowyer, C., Coastal Command at War (Ian Allen, 1979)

Chartres, J., Fly for Their Lives (Airlife, 1988)

Cox, C. B., The Steam Trawlers and Liners of Grimsby (C.B. Cox, 1989)

Halpenny, B., Action Stations No.2 The Airfields of Lincolnshire and the East Midlands (PSL, 1981)

Hodgson, M., Taylor, B., & Blake, R. Airfields of Lincolnshire Since 1912 (Midland Counties, 1984)

Hastings, M., Bomber Command (Michael Joseph, 1979)

Jones, G., Attacker: The Hudson and its Fliers (WIlliam Kimber, 1980)

Mason, F. K., The AVRO Lancaster (Aston Publications, 1989)

McIntosh, R. M. W/Cdr All Weather Mac (Macdonald, 1963)

Middlebrook, M., & Everitt, C. The Bomber Command War Diaries (Viking, 1987)

Moyle, H. The Hampden File (Air Britain,1989)

Nesbitt, R. Conyers The Strike Wings (William Kimber, 1984)

Pereira, W. D., Boat in the Blue (Line One Publications, 1985)

Pilborough, G. D., The History Of RAF Marine Craft 1918 - 1986 Vol 1 1918 - 1939 (Canimpex Publishing, 1986)

Pilborough, G. D., The History Of RAF Marine Craft 1918 - 1986
Vol 2 1939 - 1945 (Canimpex Publishing, 1987)

Pilborough, G. D., The History Of RAF Marine Craft 1918 - 1986
Vol 3 1946 - 1959 (Canimpex Publishing, 1990)

Rawlings, J. D. R. Coastal and Special Squadrons of the RAF (Janes, 1982)

Thetford, O., Aircraft of the Royal Air Force Since 1918 (Putnams, 1988)

Whittle, P. & Borrison, M., Angels Without Wings (Angley, 1966)

Magazines

Aeroplane Monthly Vol. 4 No. 10 (IPC Business Press, October 1976)
Aeroplane Monthly Vol. 8 No. 4   (IPC Business Press, April 1980)
Aeroplane Monthly Vol. 17 No. 1 (IPC Business Press, January 1989)
Aeroplane Monthly Vol. 17 No. 2 (IPC Business Press, February 1989)

Official Sources Public Record Office, Kew

Organisation of Air Sea Rescue -   AIR 2 6257

9 Squadron Operational Record Book (ORB) -   AIR 27 125

278 Squadron ORB -   AIR 27 1605 to 1608 and 1611 to 1613

280 Squadron ORB -   AIR 27 1612

22 ASRMCU ORB -   AIR 29 443

WEEKEND LEAVE
by
Stanley Naylor

Every man or woman who served in the Navy, Army and Air Force during the war years, will recall a story of how they organised a weekend leave and the unorthodox transport they used to travel to and from home. Perhaps our families were not aware of how these weekends were planned with military precision to enable us to get a few precious hours at home, only to find those plans going haywire! This is my story that is absolutely true down to the last detail, remembering that the times on the leave pass had to be strictly adhered to, especially the time to be back in camp, not one extra minute was permitted.

I was a driver in 2748 Squadron RAF Regiment that had completed a tour of duty during an horrendous winter at RAF Station Sumburgh in the Shetland Isles. We returned to the UK in the spring of 1944 and was permitted two weeks recuperation at RAF Locking near Weston-Super-Mare. It was at least a ten/fifteen-minute walk each morning for breakfast that involved passing milk churns on the roadside waiting for collection. I wonder if the farmer blamed his cows for a low milk yield during those two weeks?

The Squadron then moved to RAF Blakehill Farm near Cricklade, situated between Swindon and Cirencester in Wiltshire.

Soon after we were settled I managed to scrounge a weekend pass to operate after duty on Friday, usually 5.00 pm, to 8.00 am on the Monday. Our W.O. - who was really a 'pussy-cat', his bark being much worse than his bite gave me permission to depart from camp mid-afternoon on the Friday. This enabled me to catch RAF transport that dropped me off at Swindon Railway Station, a distance of some ten miles.

Boarding a London bound train, I arrived at Paddington and crossed the big city without incident, via the Underground Railway to Kings Cross Station.

It is worth mentioning that thousands of people used the Underground as air-raid shelters throughout the night, many of them arriving early evening. The platforms were therfore packed with sleeping bags and blankets leaving no more than four or five feet of platform for passengers leaving and departing from trains. At 11.00 pm the trains stopped running and the stations closed down leaving the sleeping occupants in peace.

A north-bound train from Kings Cross dropped me off at Peterborough in the early hours of Saturday morning, where I had to wait for the departure of the Mail Train at around 4.00 am. The darkened carriages stood in a siding and I managed to snatch a couple of hours sleep, but not as restful as it might have been. The engine being coupled to the carriages disturbed me and dim light gradually appeared outlining some fellow passengers, which I learned were on the same mission as myself.

The train eventually arrived in Boston around 5.00 am and I trudged the short distance to the Police Station that at that time was in West Street. The desk Sergeant pointed me in the direction of the bike shed, where the Kirton W.I. had generously stored a bike for the use of members of the Forces who needed transport to get home. I found the bike but the batteries were flat in the two lamps and it was still very dark.

Knowing the strict law of riding bikes without lights and not relishing hiking the six miles to home I was pondering what to do when a policeman entered the shed to collect his bike. On learning of my problem, he merely said 'Well I'm going off duty' and mounted his bike and proceeded in the direction of the town.

As soon as he was out of sight, I mounted my borrowed bike and proceeded in the opposite direction taking the low road via Wyberton and Frampton hoping the local Policeman was tucked-up nice and comfortable in bed. I finally arrived home without further incident just after 6.00 am in time to have a cup of tea with Dad, who was having breakfast after being out in the stable feeding horses.

After breakfast of eggs and bacon, I slipped into a comfortable bed between white sheets and laid my weary head on a white pillow. Sleep, however, was not restful, perhaps I was thrilled and excited at being amongst a loving family, even if it was only for a short period. Mother was convinced I was not getting enough to eat and prepared huge meals, not difficult in the country with bacon hanging on the wall, chickens at the bottom of the garden producing eggs and vegetables stored from the garden. But where did she get the ingredients for the traditional Yorkshire pudding for Sunday dinner and the trifle for tea?

Departing was never easy, perhaps more so for the family, because I found that once I was travelling the adrenaline started pumping and I was off on another adventure! I boarded the Grimsby/London express at Kirton Station just after 7.00 pm on Sunday night, bearing in mind that I needed to catch a train at Paddington Station that was departing at 1.00 am. Joining me at Kirton Station was two more RAF types, the late Roy Sentence and the late Jack Sansam, both stationed either in or on the outskirts of London.

As we neared the city the train was halted for some 20/30 minutes because the Germans had decided to pay London another visit. Eventually we crawled into the Station arriving well after 11.00 pm. A cup of tea and a sandwich seemed like a good idea and I emerged from the canteen behind Kings Cross just after midnight.

The Underground was closed, all the buses were parked in their respective depots and not a taxi in sight. "How do I get to Paddington?" I asked a policeman, who confirmed my only means of travel was on "shanks's pony". Not knowing London I asked "In which direction do I go?" He pointed me down Euston Road, Marylebone Road, Chapel Street and then Praed Street. When he mentioned the last name, my heart sank as I remembered the stories told by Cockney comrades about the 'Ladies of the Night', who patrolled this area. However, I need not have worried because I never saw a sole and therefore had no need to use my unarmed combat tactics!

It was just on 1.00 am as I entered Paddington Station and there standing between me and the platforms was two 'Snowdrops'. Having just done a brisk walk I was a prime candidate for fourteen days jankers, my overcoat was unbuttoned, cap in my right-hand and respirator slung over my left shoulder. Walking boldly up to the two RAF Police, I enquired if the train had departed for Swindon. At that moment a ticket collector was closing the gate to a platform where a passenger train was standing hissing steam. The two police shouted in unison for the gate to stay open and I was bundled onto the platform my feet hardly touching the ground.

I boarded the train as it moved from the platform to find it was crowded with standing room only in the corridor. At Reading half the passengers must have departed, most of them Americans and I easily found a corner seat and drifted into a blissful sleep.

As I awoke I realised the train was standing in a station and enquired of a passing Porter how far it was to Swindon. "Swindon" he said, "You passed it thirty miles down the line". Grabbing my respirator I dismounted from the train and asked the same porter the time of the next train back to Swindon. "8 o-clock" he replied. Now I was getting really worried, 8 o'clock was my deadline, but there was no way I could have walked the distance and been back in camp on time. I wandered into a bleak, dimly lit waiting room that had those wooden seats around the walls and a plain wooden table in the centre and at that point I was certain I was still a prime candidate for some jankers.

The passenger train moved out of the station and there standing on the opposite line was a goods train. Thinking on the hoof there might be a slim chance of a lift, I raced over the footbridge and down the side of the trucks to the engine. On hearing my appeal for a lift, the driver asked to see my rail ticket and pass, both confirmed my story and I was invited to climb aboard the engine. The fireman was instructed to stop taking on anymore water and the goods train started on its journey towards Swindon. This really was something to be savoured, but I was in no mood to enjoy the experience.

It was daylight as we approached Swindon, the time was about 7.00 am, leaving me one hour to travel some ten miles. The driver slowed as we entered the outskirts of the town allowing me to jump off the engine. I was instructed to walk down the road ahead of me and take the first left turn, which was the road to Cricklade. On turning the corner I saw a Wimpy lorry loading workmen.

Now RAF Blakehill Farm had just been constructed by Wimpy and the workmen were finishing off a few jobs. The answer was "Yes" to my question if they were going to Blakehill and "Yes" I could have a lift. Suffice to say the lorry dropped me at the Guardroom with only a few minutes of my weekend leave to spare. After leaving the Guardroom I strolled casually over to the billet, the panic was now over, or so I thought. As I entered the billet, which was a Nissen Hut, that very nice WO followed me through the door and said in a very loud voice "Ah Naylor, you've made it by the skin of your teeth, I want you at work in half-an-hour". A lovely man, really!

The reader may wonder if the weekend had been worth all the hassle of travelling to and from home. Just to recap, travelling time home was fifteen hours, 3.00 pm on Friday to 6.00 am on Saturday. Thirty-seven hours at home, 6.00 am on Saturday to 7.00 pm on Sunday. Travelling on the return journey was thirteen hours, 7.00 pm on Sunday to 8.00 am on Monday. The answer is an emphatic YES, because it was some eighteen months before I managed to get home on fourteen days leave in November 1945, plus a week travelling to and from Germany. But that is another story that started just over fifty-five years of married life!

Stanley Naylor, 2001

D-DAY

They fought for freedom. They gave their lives so others might live theirs free from the yoke of fascism.
Today we salute the heroes of D-Day, the men who went to war to liberate the world from Nazi tyranny.
Plucked from civvy street and plunged into the fury of battle, they were ordinary men who showed extraordinary courage.

Sunday Mirror, 22nd May 1994

A PRAYER FOR YOU

You told me not to worry,
   That you'd always make it through.
You said to keep my chin up,
   And just say a prayer for you.

The young think they're immortal,
   With death far out of sight.
But not for such as you though,
   Death flew with you each night.

And Ops' would be to Berlin,
   Or Dortmund or Cologne.
Those fearful hours of hoping,
   Each night I slept alone.

But many nights were sleepless,
   And I would lay forlorn.
For fate could keep me waiting,
   Till another day was born.

But then the roar of Merlin's,
   Would boom across the sky.
I'd try to count each Lanc' safe home,
   More often though I'd cry.

Then one morn they came to tell me,
   That you were overdue;
But later it was 'Missing',
   For S-Sugar and her crew.

Now my crying is long over,
   Though I'll always know the pain.
And my prayers will ever be for you,
   For you'll not come home again.

© *John R. Walsh, 1987*

UNITED STATES ARMY AIR FORCE

At the beginning of the Second World War, most US citizens didn't want to get involved in another European conflict, yet several hundred risked losing their citizenship by volunteering to serve with British Forces. Many flew with the Royal Air Force special 'Eagle Squadrons' in Fighter Command, while non-uniformed engineers and medics came over and helped on several British bases - purely on the 'buddy principal'. Also in December 1940 Congress agreed to supply on Lend Lease the arms and vehicles Britain so urgently needed.

Then Japan's assault on the US naval base at Pearl Harbour on 7th December 1941, causing massive destruction, resulted in the US declaring war on Japan and four days later on Germany and Italy. On 8th December President Roosevelt cabled Winston Churchill; "Today all of us are in the same boat with you . . . and it is a ship which will not and can not be sunk". After this Churchill admitted he "went to bed and slept the sleep of the saved and thankful".

By the spring of 1942 US troops landings in Britain were well under way and all summer passenger liners including 'Queen Elizabeth' and 'Queen Mary' zig-zagged across the Atlantic, dodging U-boats and carrying up to 18,000 soldiers and airmen at a time. While many of the military went to North Africa, about 30,000 USAAF spent their first winter on British bases, mostly in a flat farming area near to Europe - East Anglia.

The only time I was involved with any Americans was boarding a US LST (landing ship tank) at Tilbury on the River Thames in 1944, when 2831 Squadron, RAF Regiment, was transported complete with vehicles to Ostend in Belgium. We had already been on board a British Naval LST and spent a night anchored in the mouth of the Thames in line with Southend Pier. I must say that Navy Rum ensures a good night's sleep! Then next morning we returned to Tilbury and the bell-tented village at Grays in Essex and a few more nights listening to the buzzing of the Doodle-Bugs passing over head.

There was no Rum on the US LST, but we were on board for Sunday lunch. We were aware that the GI's enjoyed exceedingly good food, but we really got a surprise when lunch was served during the journey. No such thing as roast beef and Yorkshire pudding, tinned chicken was on the menu. We used our mess-tins, oblong shaped tins with handles, but we didn't know where the main course finished and the sweet started. Suffice to say that we emerged from the galley with tins piled high with sumptuous food, the like we had never seen before and never saw again.

It was the USAAF that had the most permanent association with the UK during the Second World War and whose members generally made the most impression on the British population. Some of them not only served here for three full years, but at the same location. By June 1943 the number of US airmen in Britain was over 100,000 and by D-Day peaked at 436,000. The largest concentration was in the greater East Anglian area where most of the 8th Air Force and some of the 9th were located on near a hundred bases.

In terms of men and machines, the 8th Air Force of the Second World War was the largest air striking force ever committed to battle. It could despatch 3,000 bombers and fighters on a single day's operation, which meant that more than 20,000 young men would take to the sky and go out to battle from East Anglia. The despatch of these operations presented a never to be forgotten spectacle for people who lived in the region, although at the time it became almost commonplace. Apart from the dramatic sights in the sky, the noise from thousands of unsilenced aero engines flooded the countryside; rare were the occasions when the throb and drone were absent.

Nearly a quarter of a million men and women were serving with the 8th at peak inventory and during the course of its units stay in the United Kingdom - which extended to nearly four years in some cases - it is estimated a total of 350,000 personnel came under its direction.

The 9th Air Force was re-formed in England in October 1943 after a period of service in the Middle East and was mainly based in Essex. Specially constructed Advanced Landing Grounds in Kent were made in order to lengthen dwell times over France before and during the invasion. It also provided valuable experience for the troops of the engineer aviation battalions, many of whom were among the first members of the 9th Air Force to land in Normandy on D-Day.

Apart from its strike aircraft, the 9th Air Force was the operator of the most formidable troop-carrying force ever assembled. On D-Day no less than 56 squadrons in fourteen troop carrier groups were in action carrying paratroops or towing gliders. This force, based on airfields in Lincolnshire, Nottinghamshire, Wiltshire, Somerset and Devon, later took part in the airborne operations to Arnhem.

As in any military formation, the work put in by the personnel behind the scenes, usually unrecorded, was invaluable. To deal with the massive task of provisioning, servicing, assembly and generally making sure that the 9th Air Force functioned properly, IX Air Force Service Command was formed. Among its many tasks were the assembly of aircraft shipped over the Atlantic into British ports and assembly of over 4,000 CG-4 gliders, each of which arrived in five large packing cases. The record for glider assembly was 100 in a single day. IX Air Force Service Command also set up a series of Tactical Air Depots, where aircraft of specific types were given major overhauls.

During the 25 months of its existence, the 9th grew from a tiny nucleus to over 200,000 personnel in 45 combat groups and a vast selection of non-combat units, flying over 1,100 bomber aircraft, a huge number of fighters and 3,000 troop-carrying aircraft. The men and women who served in the 9th Air Force can rightly be proud of their efforts and attainments.

Aircraft operated by the 8th and 9th Air Force included B-17 Fortresses; B-24 Liberators; P-47 Thunderbolts; P-38 Lightnings; A-20 Bostons; B-26 Marauders; P-51 Mustangs; C-47 Skytrains and the gliders were mainly Waco CG-4s, plus a number of British-built Horsas.

Information for the above story has been gleaned from the "Official Souvenir Guide of the Reunion 1942 - 1992", by kind permission of the East of England Tourist Board, for which I am most grateful.

Glancy's Bag

Some basic research leads to a story of terror over Germany.

In 1995, 388th Collection Curators, David Sarson and Alan Tebbell, bought at auction an un-opened military travel bag once belonging to E L Glancy of the USAAF 388th Bombardment Group. The bag had been stored in an East Anglia attic for 50 years. The question of why Glancy left it behind was solved when his name was found on a 388th casualty list. But no other information on Glancy could be found. The two curators sought help from the 388th Bombardment Group Association in the United States, which led them to Roy Barry of Milwaukee, Wisconsin.

What follows is a letter from Barry to the curators of the 388th Collection, recounting not only Glancy's death, but also Barry's own harrowing tale of survival.

The letter:

"On 9th April 1945 I was part of the B-17 heavy bomb crew whose mission and target that day was the railroad marshalling yards at Munich, Germany. My enlisted rank was Staff Sergeant and my crew position on the aircraft was Sperry Lower Ball Turret Operator".

"Our ship's name was 'Lil' Tammara', named after our ship Commander's newly born daughter. Our ship Commander, 1st Lt. Rex E Barwick, was killed instantly on that Munich 'trip' by a large chunk of flak which upon exploding hit him in the abdomen and literally cut him in half".

"Because our regular crew member Bombardier had been assigned for that mission as a Lead Bombardier in our Group Commander's ship, we were assigned a fill-in, Togglier Sgt Glancy".

"Leaving the target area over the railyard at Munich, as we banked away, we were hit with two direct flak bursts, large fragments of which tore open our Plexiglass nose and knocked out our Number 3 (right in-board) engine".

"A large shell fragment entered our nose compartment, passing through Glancy's body and, according to our navigator who was only a few feet away from Glancy when he was hit, Glancy was mortally wounded and was lucky to have got out of the ship".

"Our navigator himself was trapped in the control cables up in the nose section and was finally sucked out by the ship's slip stream from another hole blown in the engine side of the nose. Our navigator speculated that the flak fragment that travelled through Glancy's body also went on to go through our pilot's body, killing him also".

"The shell fragments that tore our Plexiglass nose apart created gaping holes in the fuselage, also severing gasoline lines leading from our wings to our engines and caught fire when our electrical cables were severed by the flying flak fragments and short circuited, creating sparks. The fuel spewing about was ignited, along with oil and oxygen leaking from severed lines to the extent that the heat generated caused fuselage structural members to melt".

"Because our source of on-board electricity had been shut off by flak damage, my lower ball turret became inoperative from lack of power and I could not rotate my turret to remove myself from inside, and for a time was trapped until I could dislodge the cranks that are used for just such loss-of-power emergencies, finally forcing my turret into such a position that I could partially open the escape and entry door and force my way into the ship's fuselage".

"I attempted to go forward through the radio room and bomb bay, but all I saw was a solid wall of roaring flame, so I went to the waste exit door, which had already been removed by other crew members before they parachuted out. I leapt and made my jump earthwards from 24,000 feet. It is my understanding that our ship crash landed - a flaming total wreck - about 15 miles west of Munich, with our pilot dead at the controls".

"His wallet was found by German soldiers and bore his name embossed in gold. We were shown the wallet later at Luftwaffe Headquarters in Munich".

"Upon landing, I was knocked unconscious for a time and fractured my right ankle".

"When I came to, a Luftwaffe major in dress blues was standing next to me with his pistol out. He was holding some civilians at bay and telling them I was a prisoner of war. It turned out they wanted to kill me, so I owe my life to that Luftwaffe pilot".

"As we walked together towards the centre of Munich he explained to me that he was a jet fighter pilot who flew the new ME262".

"A similar escape took place on the outskirts of Munich when another Luftwaffe pilot found our co-pilot, 2nd Lt Warren C Perkins, lying on the ground unconscious, still strapped to his parachute harness and about to be shot by SS troopers".

"The Luftwaffe pilot outranked the SS and ordered them away, helped our pilot off with his chute harness and took him prisoner".

"He then commandeered a German army truck and had him conveyed to a local hospital to be treated for his broken arm".

"While the Luftwaffe major took me into custody and kept the civilians at bay with his pistol. I spotted out of the corner of my eye our radio man and waist gunner attempting to crawl from around a building about a half-block away".

"I was watching when, as the two of them rounded the corner of the building, two SS men armed with machine guns came from the back of the building and shot and killed them. I attempted to go to their aid but the Major restrained me and said, 'Nein, they ist kaput, Dead'".

"Shortly after returning home after the war, I received a letter of inquiry from Glancy's sister in New Jersey asking me what happened to her brother. She did not believe the war department that her brother was dead. I told her that he had indeed been killed, or at least mortally wounded, even if he did escape our flaming ship".

"On reading the article on the jacket and bag in the 388th newsletter, I was astonished to see the name of Earl Glancy. He did fly with us on that fateful mission. We had been looking forward to packing up and going home to the States after three more trips".

"It is my understanding that Glancy was on his second tour of flying duty. We understood from him that he often lived off base and stayed with some civilian folk in Thetford".

Roy Barry
Milwaukee, Wisconsin
561st Sqdn 388th BG

Research Notes:

The Luftwaffe pilot who saved Lt Warren Perkins life on that fateful day in April 1945, was Werner P Roell, who now lives in Switzerland and operates a successful international engineering company.

Roy Barry heard the news of Earl Glancy's death from his navigator when they met after capture at the SS-Wehrmacht and Luftwaffe Headquarters in Munich.

The only two survivors of the *'Lil' Tammara'* crew now are Roy Barry and Floyd E Pernu, Tail Gunner, of Pastorville, California.

This story has been included by kind permission of David Sarson, Curator of the 388th Collection, dedicated to preserving the history and memories of the men who lived and fought from Knettishall, Station 136, during the Second World War.

For further details of the 388th Collection, contact David Sarson at Hillside Farm, Market Weston, Suffolk, IP22 2NX, UK. (See advertisement at the back of the book).

The only airworthy B-17 in the UK is Boeing B-17G Flying Fortress, known as 'Sally B', and is based at the Imperial War Museum at Duxford, near Cambridge. 'Sally B', flies as a memorial to the 79,000 allied airmen who lost their lives in Europe in World War II.

For further information please contact: B-17 Preservation Ltd, PO Box 92, Bury St Edmunds, Suffolk, IP28 8RR. Tel: 01638 720304.

Foot-note:

Recent research has discovered that Sgt Glancy was actually shot by the Germans, even though he had parachuted safely from his stricken aircraft. His body was returned to the USA on the 26th of January 1948 and was honoured with a military funeral.

**In Memoriam and
The Royal British Legion
"Act of Homage".**

They shall grow not old, as we that are left grow old;
Age shall not weary them, nor the years condemn.
At the going down of the sun and in the morning,
We will remember them.

This is the middle verse of seven verses from a poem 'For The Fallen',
by Laurence Binyon.

BEAUFIGHTER VERSUS DORNIER

The night of the eighth of May 1941 was a very bright moonlight night. P/O D.W. Thompson with P/O Britain as his A1 operator was ordered out on patrol from RAF Wittering at 23.35 hrs. They took off in a Beaufighter of A Flight, 25 Squadron and were vectored south of Digby. At 14,000 feet and north of the Wash they picked up a bleep on their radar. They set chase that lasted for about three minutes. In front of them, but slightly below and some 400 yards away at approximately 13,000 feet, the silhouette of an enemy aircraft could be seen. It stood out stark and clear in the bright moonlight on the cloud layer around 6,000 feet below them. Both P/O Thompson and P/O Britain agreed it was a Dornier 215. The aircraft in fact, was a Dornier 17 ZK10, an early Night Fighter that was one of only ten built.

P/O Thompson realised he was approaching the enemy too fast and throttled back causing flames to appear from the engine's exhausts. Although up-moon of the enemy aircraft the approaching Beaufighter had been seen and as P/O Thompson fired a one-second-burst of tracer the German managed to avoid them.

The three crew on board the Dornier that night were Pilot F.W. Wilheim Lettermeier, his Wireless Operator Unft Georg Herden and Uffz Herbert Thomas. Lettermeier was on his first Night Fighter combat mission. Herbert Thomas, a more experienced flier with about forty missions to his credit since July 1940, had been assigned the task of training the young Pilots on their first few trips. They were all from the 2/NIG2 Night Fighter Sqdn from Gilze Rijen. The Dornier was a conversion from the DO 17 bomber and fitted with the early Liechtenstein radar and canon, coded R4+GK and Wrk No. 2843.

After avoiding the first attack by a steep turn to port, the pilot, thinking he had lost the Beaufighter, returned to a straight course again, unaware that P/O Thompson's Beaufighter had picked them up and was closing in for the kill! Thompson, now only approximately a hundred yards away, fired a short burst from below hitting the starboard engine. With the Dornier diving to port, that engine was then hit which immediately burst into flames and the aircraft started to spiral down. Inside the

Dornier the crew had all been slightly injured by flying splinters but were still able to carry out practical procedure taken in such an event: - ignition out, petrol cock off and full throttle to clear the remaining petrol in the pipes. Lettermeier and Thomas pulled hard on the control column but were unable to correct the spiral dive. Herbert Thomas gave the order to bail out and saw Georg Herden jettison his cover.

What happened during the next few minutes was very vague, as Thomas recalled. He felt a terrific knock, his senses became dimmed but was aware of the heat all around him and felt a lot of pain. Suddenly everything went quiet until the pain shot through him again, even though it seemed as if he had been drugged. Thomas believes that with the canopy gone he was dragged out of the aircraft by suction and thrown against the tailplane. His parachute harness may have caught some part of the tail as the straps were later found to be slightly torn. Without realising it, he must have pulled the ripcord and the opening chute had dragged him clear of the falling aircraft.

Thomas did not know where he was or how long he had been lying on the ground. On regaining consciousness he believed he was in heaven, his parachute had covered him completely and the bright moonlight shining through the chute gave him that impression. He then heard voices which seemed very distant, but people had arrived and were standing around him. Someone may have pushed a Woodbine between his lips. He soon found himself sat in a car with George Herden next to him. They were in the charge of the local constable, P C Cutts. They were told that Lettermeier had not survived the crash. In fact, he had bailed out but the Dornier was too low and he was found about one hundred yards from the crash site.

Thomas next remembers waking up on the operating table and being embarrassed as a young nurse cut off his flying suit and uniform. After he came out of the anaesthetic he found himself encased in plaster. Beside him sat a heavily armed soldier, who later became a good friend, especially because of his Woodbines which he generously shared with Thomas. The friendship was soon to end, as escape was impossible the guard was assigned to other duties. Thomas received quite good treatment in the hospital, inspite of bring cursed as the 'damned German pilot' by the doctors and nurses. He was in a ward hidden by a screen around his bed, that was removed one Sunday making him the talking point of the hospital visitors. He remembers one little boy placing a toffee on his bed covers.

After two or three months Thomas was moved to No. 4 Military Hospital in Knutsford, Cheshire. He was eventually repatriated to Germany, as his injuries were considered too severe to let him take any active part in the War.

Forty-three years after this event, the Lincolnshire Aircraft Recovery Group (LARG), located the final resting place of Herbert Thomas's rare Dornier 17ZK on the bank of Medlam Drain near Short's Corner, Carrington, Boston. After obtaining the relevant permission from both the MOD and the landowners, LARG set about recovering the remains of the aircraft. A preliminary search of the site with metal detectors proved almost fruitless with only a few fragments of metal being found. This was later found to be due to the fact the aircraft had crashed into a riverbank, which had in later years been levelled off, so removing any surface wreckage that may have been there.

It was on an August morning in 1984 that the LARG turned up at the crash site with a Hymac mechanical digger and started the recovery.

At a depth of about fifteen feet the first signs of the aircraft was found as Glycol and oil seeped into the hole. Amongst the first large pieces of wreckage to be recovered was the complete and intact tail wheel tyre and tube. The tube was later taken to a local garage and inflated and has remained inflated ever since.

As the dig continued, vast amounts of wreckage were uncovered. At a final depth of some thirty-five feet, part of the reduction gear was pulled out. Amongst the items recovered were approximately one third of one of the Bramo Fafnir engines, two MG 17 machine guns, a badly torn dingy and survival kit complete with flare pistol and flares. Also found in the wreckage was a briefcase, which belonged to Georg Herden. In the contents was found navigational maps and code books, his 'kappi' (forage cap) and a handkerchief with his initials on it.

In April 1986 LARG group members met Herbert Thomas at the Hendon Aircraft Museum, London, where they presented him with some pieces of his Dornier, including the ignition keys.

On the 17th July 1987, a unique occasion took place at RAF Coningsby when two World War II combatants met again, just forty-six years after they first met over the skies of Lincolnshire.

Herbert Thomas, now sixty-four years of age, a German airman returned to England to collect some more of the remains of his Dornier 17ZK10 Night Fighter aircraft, which had been recovered by LARG in 1984. To present the wreckage to him was the man that shot him down back in 1941, P/O Dennis Britain Ex. RAF now aged eighty-five years.

The Lincolnshire Aircraft Recovery Group and Royal Air Force, Coningsby, arranged the presentation. They were hosts to some fifty people, including sixteen wartime German Airmen from the Association of Former Nightfighter Groups. Mr Castle-Miller, a wartime Intelligence Officer from No. 25 RAF Squadron; Mr 'Rick' Pilcher, the surgeon who operated on Herr Thomas and Mr Sargent, son of the Home Guard who first captured him.

A tour of RAF Coningsby was organised and the German Air Force arranged for a Dornier 28 to collect the Dornier 17 wreckage, which was escorted by two Phantom Jets.

Produced by kind permission of David Stubley, LARG

THE MAIL TRAIN
by
Jim Jackson

Some time ago we were reminiscing about the railway journeys made while we were in the RAF. Those who lived in Boston at the time will recall coming home on leave and forty-eight's via Peterborough - nearly always on the 'Mail Train'.

This usually meant that you had managed to get to Peterborough from the far ends of the country only to find that the last train of the evening for Boston had left and you had to wait for the first one of the next day. The carriages would be standing cold and empty in the blacked-out station, waiting for the train from London with the day's newspapers and mail for Spalding, Boston and North Lincolnshire up to Grimsby.

On being coupled to an engine the train become dimly lit, though never really warmed. Gradually more bods would arrive and occupy the vacant seats until all compartments were full and eventually in the early hours of the morning the train left Peterborough North heading for home but stopping at every wayside station.

Many will have memories of the Mail Train - like the matelot whose ship was just home from a tour in the Pacific; he neglected to tell anyone he wanted to get off at Boston and woke in a siding at Cleethorpes!

The journey I recall most on the Mail Train was really rather sad - as the compartment filled up we talked and discovered who our travelling companions were. I remember some of them - like the sailor going to join a minesweeper at Grimsby, an Army bod coming home on leave like myself, and an RAF Corporal returning from leave to RAF Station Coningsby.

Eventually the shadowy figure on the platform blew his whistle and swung his lamp and the train started to move. At the last minute a breathless girl in civvies jumped into our compartment and squeezed into the space of the seat next to the Corporal. As the carriage lights brightened we could make out that she would have appeared quite pretty if she had been in smarter clothes and not looking so tired-eyed.

I assumed that she might have just finished a shift in a factory from her appearance and the fact that she soon dropped off to sleep with her head on the Corporal's shoulder. After a few minutes she became quite restless and started mumbling in her sleep - 'We must get another forty made this week - beat the target - another forty more -'

Gradually she became quiet, but remained still with her head on his shoulder, and we resumed our previous talk which had turned to the subject of air raids on our cities. This had set off the Corporal, who was going into gory details of the mayhem of one particular direct hit on one of the London street markets, where there were many civilian casualties.

As he was carrying on at great length the girl started gently sobbing, although she still appeared to be a sleep. He was continuing with his story and seemed to relish describing the disaster when she suddenly shot up out of the seat and stumbled out into the corridor with a cry - 'My mother and father were killed in that raid!'

She didn't come back and nobody talked much after that, least of all the Corporal.

A C J Jackson, Ex. RAF

No. 4 RAF HOSPITAL RAUCEBY

by

Mrs Gwyneth Stratten

In 1939 as war clouds gathered it was realised that the small, well-equipped hospital at RAF Cranwell would be inadequate to cope with the reception and treatment of patients on a large scale. On April 11th 1940, the Cranwell staff and patients took over the new (then) admissions unit which we knew as Orchard House. Extensive alterations were made which included the equipping of two operating theatres.

In June the same year an urgent request was made for further accommodation. Consultations between the Hospital Committee, the board of Control, Ministry of Health and the Air Ministry led to the evacuation of the main hospital building and the Nurses Home.

No. 4 Hospital RAF Rauceby had been planned as one of the principal RAF Hospitals and with hindsight we realise that its position was of vital importance to provide medical services for the multitude of RAF Stations that eventually covered Lincolnshire and beyond.

The very nature of the warfare meant that many of the crew-members were not only physically injured but also badly burnt. Rauceby so often became the first step on the long and painful road to recovery.

We must acknowledge the pioneering work of the resident surgeon, Sqd. Ldr. Fenton Braithwaite and his burns team and the surgeons and staff of the adjacent Orthopedic Unit.

Sir Archibald McIndoe, whom everyone associates with East Grinstead and the Guinea Pig Club, also visited and operated at RAF Rauceby. A number of cases were transferred to East Grinstead from RAF Rauceby for further surgery.

At the height of the war there were some one thousand beds in use and another one thousand in store to be used in the event of invasion or extensive bombing.

That the hospital was busy can be seen by the statistics – for example, in 1943, nearly 4,400 operations were performed and over 23,000 cases treated. Men and women of all nationalities passed through these portals and it became a familiar sight to see patients in the locality in their ill-fitting uniform.

A number of young men, who became legends in their own lifetimes, had occasion to be patients of Rauceby. For instance:-

Wing Commander Guy Gibson V.C., who was here shortly before he went on his last fatal mission; Flight Sergeant John Hannah who won his V.C., at the age of eighteen in 1940, (sadly, he was discharged from the RAF in 1942 and died in 1947); Air Chief Marshal Sir Augustus Walker, who, as Commanding Officer at Syerston, lost an arm in an airfield accident.

Happy (albeit painful) memories abound from the most exalted rank to the lowliest 'erk'. Moral was high and spirits lightened by the provision of entertainment in the form of shows and dances which were held weekly. Many famous names trod the boards of Rauceby stage and the weekly dances with music provided by the hospital's own dance band 'The Medicos', were popular with both those at the hospital and local residents.

Rauceby fortunately escaped damage at the hands of the enemy but accidentally suffered severe damage to its ballroom. On Whit-Monday night in 1945 a fire was discovered at 3.00 am. This must have been burning for several hours, as the wood panelling and highly polished floors were well alight. Despite the efforts of hospital and local fire brigades the room was completely gutted. It did not rise from the flames until 1948.

The feeling of close companionship shared by the medical staff led to the formation of a unique club simply known as "The RAUCEBY CLUB". It was formed by Wg. Cdr. Eric Jewsbury and included all medical staff who had worked or had connections with RAF Hospital Rauceby. Its membership list reads as a "Who's Who" of the medical profession as many of these doctors and surgeons went on to achieve eminence in their particular fields. The Club was unique in that it was the only one of its kind ever formed. It's annual dinners, which continued well into the 1980's, became legendary.

RAF Hospital Rauceby was in existence for a comparatively short period (1940 to 1947) and whilst much of the work carried out had been routine, a fair amount had been, by the nature of the injuries sustained, both experimental and life saving. Many of the techniques developed then are still in use today.

The RAF Hospital has been a focal point during a unique period of Lincolnshire history and many more people had cause to be grateful for its existence. All that is left are memories and records in writing with photographs that bear silent witness to the bravery and fortitude of the patients and the humanity and skills of the staff.

LET US NOT FORGET!

Produced by kind permission of Mrs Gwyneth Stratten

These are the last six lines from the poem:
'In Flanders Fields'

Take up your quarrel with the foe;
To you from failing hands we throw
The torch; be yours to hold it high,
If ye break faith with us who die
We shall not sleep, though poppies grow
In Flanders fields.

By Colonel John McCrae, a Canadian medical officer, 1915.

HIGH FLIGHT

Oh! I have slipped the surly bonds of earth
And danced the skies on laughter-silvered wings;
Sunward I've climbed, and joined the tumbling mirth
Of sun split clouds - and done a hundred things
You have not dreamed of -
        wheeled and soured and swung
High in the sunlit silence. Hov'ring there,
I've chased the shouting wind along, and flung
My eager craft through footless halls of air.
Up, up the long delirious, burning blue,
I've topped the windswept heights with easy grace,
Where never lark, or even eagle flew.
And, while with silent lifting mind I've trod
The high untrespassed sanctity of space,
Put out my hand and touched the face of God.

Pilot Officer - John Gillespie Magee, Jnr. RCAF 1941

John Magee Jnr was born in China in June 1922. His parents were missionaries, English mother - American father. John was in America at the beginning of the 1939 - 1945 War, he joined the Canadian Air Force and trained as a pilot. On completion of his training, PO Magee joined No. 412 Canadian Squadron at RAF Digby in the UK. Unfortunately on 11th December 1941 when Magee was returning from a patrol and descending through cloud, his Spitfire collided with another aircraft from RAF Cranwell, killing both pilots. Pilot Officer John Gillespie Magee Jnr. is buried beside a number of other airmen in Scopwick Cemetery, two miles from Digby, Lincolnshire.

LANCASTER MEMORIAL
Bishop's Farm, Sibsey Northlands
Boston, Lincolnshire

This is the story that I have compiled that includes eye witness accounts of the Lancaster Bomber aircraft that crashed approximately 3.30p.m. on 29th January 1943.

The aircraft involved was a new four engine Lancaster Mk. III Bomber ED503 with only eighty-five minutes flying time recorded. The Lancaster was attached to No. 9 Squadron at RAF Waddington in Lincolnshire. However, after a bombing mission had been cancelled, the aircraft was operating from RAF Coningsby on an engine and airframe test flight incorporating a fighter affiliation exercise. Hence the reason for the presence of a Spitfire fighter aircraft.

It was also understood that because the aircraft was flying locally there was no need for a navigator. However, at the Service on Sunday 4th October 1998, a relative of one of the crew informed me the navigator failed to make the flight and one of the six crew members was acting as navigator. Whatever the reason for the regular navigator missing the flight, it most certainly saved his life. But I wonder where he is today and what his thoughts must be on this untimely crash?

It is reported there was no sign of a collision and the Lancaster subsequently nose-dived into the ground causing a massive explosion and a fireball erupted. The Spitfire made one pass over the crash site and then headed off in the direction of RAF Coningsby.

The following information has been gleaned from eye witnesses.

<u>Thomas (Tom) Henry and Nora Wilson.</u>

Tom was born 10th March 1922 and joined the Royal Air Force (RAF) in the spring of 1941. Like myself, after six weeks elementary training, Tom was drafted to a RAF Station as a GD, which we all assumed was General Duties but was in fact Ground Defence. The name was then changed to GG (Ground Gunner) and on 1st February 1942 all GG

Squadrons automatically formed the Royal Air Force Regiment.

In January 1943 Tom was granted leave to marry Nora and the ceremony took place at Skegness on Wednesday 27th January. The following day, Thursday 28th the newly married couple moved to Stickney.

The afternoon of 29th January 1943 was dry, sunny, very warm and visibility was good. Tom and Nora were therefore encouraged to go for a walk and observed a Lancaster Bomber aircraft flying south/easterly from the direction of RAF Coningsby. They also noted a Spitfire darting around the aircraft as if in mock attack. Although large aircraft was a familiar sight in the area, this magnificent Lancaster held their gaze as it continued on a low level flight undisturbed by the manoeuvring Spitfire. Then as the small aircraft retreated in the direction of Boston, the Lancaster commenced to climb. From Tom's daily experience of seeing heavy aircraft take the air, this was a routine climb and nothing appeared abnormal. However, no sooner had this large aircraft commenced to climb and there was no visible reason for doing so, it nose-dived to its final resting-place.

Tom was wheeling his cycle, for whatever reason, and fearing the worst, raced to the crash site and was second on the scene. He found the aircraft was a fireball with bullets popping off all over the area making any rescue virtually impossible. It would seem the plane had changed direction in the fall and was facing north in its crashed position, but Tom and Nora assured me it was flying in a south/easterly direction prior to the disaster. Tom was in RAF uniform and stayed at the scene for some considerable time. When fire and ambulance crews arrived he returned to Stickney.

<u>Bill Bursnell</u>

First on the scene was the late Bill Bursnell who was working in his shirt sleeves only a short distance from where the aircraft crashed. Bill related his version of the crash to Bert Barrack that corresponds to the facts given to me by Tom Wilson.

John Edward 'Ted' Callaby

Ted was born on 5th March 1921 and on 29th January 1943 was working as second horseman on the farm (now demolished) at West Houses, Sibsey Northlands, owned by Alderman Charles Fleet.

Ted states it was a lovely sunny afternoon with almost a cloudless sky as he conveyed pea straw from a stack in the corner of the nine-acre field where the plane crashed. On the short journey to the farm, Ted had observed what he described as a low-flying Lancaster approaching from the direction of RAF Coningsby. He stated this was nothing out-of-the-ordinary because aircraft were often passing over the area and therefore did not attract too much attention. He had barely arrived at the farm with a loaded cart when he heard a terrific crash. Looking in the direction of the field he had just vacated, Ted was astonished to see the Lancaster he had seen airborne only minutes before had nose-dived in the ground and was engulfed in flames with plumes of black smoke pouring skywards. The startled horses demanded Ted's attention and therefore he was unable to go to the aircraft. In his view, however, no one aboard the aircraft could have survived such a horrific crash.

Ted continued his story stating that an armed guard duly arrived and was billeted on the farm. Not only were they involved in guard duties for some 12/14 days, but also helped to collect all the debris that was scattered over a large area that Ted conveyed with his horses and cart to the farm. When the salvage operation was complete, a vehicle that Ted described as a very long RAF lorry collected all the surface debris that had been stored at the farm. The lorry would no doubt be what we knew in the RAF as a 'Queen Mary'.

The local Fire Brigade tried for two days to pump the crater clear of water, but it refilled as fast as it was pumped out. Therefore owing to the excessive amount of water and silted soil at a depth of several feet, it became an impossible task to recover five of the bodies. Only the body of Sergeant Thomas Wishart, RAF VR No. 969171 aged 25 years, the rear gunner, was recovered and is buried in his home town of Dalkieth, Scotland.

The Officer Commanding No. 9 RAF Squadron attempted to have the site of the crash consecrated and a memorial erected by the War Graves Commission, which was not successful.

It was after the War that the families of the five-crew members buried in this Fenland arable field on Bishop's Farm, approached the owner, who was as already stated, Alderman Charles Fleet, with the intention of having a memorial erected on the site. Mr Brown, a relative of one of the crew members, informs me that Alderman Charles Fleet was very generous in offering as much as an acre on which a Memorial could be erected. Because it would not have been practical to maintain such a large plot of land, the families agreed to accept a smaller plot. Subsequently a Memorial was erected and consecrated in 1947 that marks the spot where our five comrades are resting in peace.

The present owners are Messrs Grant Brothers who are very co-operative and unstinting in their help, for which the families, RAF Coningsby, the RBL and RAFA members are most grateful.

(Because the Memorial is on private property, would you please observe the Country Code of preserving crops. Permission should therefore be obtained from the farmers before entering their field. Thank You!)

The five names engraved on the Memorial are:

Pilot   Flight Lieutenant (Flt. Lt) Robert Frood Lind, RAF. VR. No. 123690 aged 25 years.

Bomb Aimer   Pilot Officer (P.O.) Charles Wilford Hurman Cocks, RAF. VR. No. 1391459 aged 34 years.

Air Gunner   Sergeant (Sgt) Donald Arthur Brown, RAF. VR. No. 1576940 aged 20 years.

Wireless Operator   Sergeant (Sgt) Thomas Joseph Henry, RAF. VR. No. 1021115, age not known.
(Incidentally: RAF - Royal Air Force and VR - Volunteer Reserve)

Flight Engineer   Sergeant (Sgt) John Doran, RAF. No. 523425, age not known, but his number suggests that he enlisted prior to September 1939 and a pre-war pilot has confirmed it is a pre-war number.

An annual service takes place at 2.30 pm on the first Sunday in October that now attracts over one hundred people from all walks of life who wish to remember this gallant crew. Attending each year is the resident Commanding Officer at RAF Coningsby, the resident Padre conducts this unique outdoor service and the annually elected Mayor and Mayoress of Boston also pay their respects.

Bert Barrack has mentioned his experience of a peaceful atmosphere during his many visits to this site. I can also say I have experienced the same feeling of tranquillity, especially on the afternoon of 5th October 1998, when securing wreaths to prevent them blowing away. There was no other person in sight, not a sound, not a bird singing or even a breath of wind. Some people might refer to it as being eerie, but I agree with Bert, it has a real peaceful atmosphere. I have experienced the same peaceful feeling when visiting many cemeteries on my tours of the Somme in Northern France and Ypres in Belgium.

However, on this Monday my thoughts were with the five air crew resting in peace beneath this unique Memorial that stands proudly in an arable field in this flat, but picturesque English countryside.

Stanley Naylor, 2001

Alex Palmer, Sunday Mirror 22nd May 1994, reminds us that on D-Day each soldier carried enough food and water for 24 hours, but it was three days before the Catering Corps could brew up a cup of tea. Interestingly he says that most US soldiers and French Resistance Fighters first tasted tea on the Normandy beaches.

LANCASTER MEMORIAL
(Sibsey Northlands)

Lancaster, the bomber of great might,
    On a fighter affiliation flight.
With a Spitfire flying so high,
    Why did you fall so fast from the sky?

Five brave and noble men,
    Who did not choose their grave in the Fen.
Whose names are carved on this stone,
    Never more will they ever roam.

They shared a common bond,
    Throughout their few short years, long gone.
They were young laughing together,
    Now lay here in peace for ever.

One other member of the crew,
    Also shared that bond so true.
His grave is in Dalkieth,
    Often mentioned, if only brief.

We travel down the muddy track,
    Every year we vow to come back.
To honour these six gallant men,
    For: 'WE WILL REMEMBER THEM'.

© *Stanley Naylor, August 1999*

Mr Geoff Hadfield, BEM., 97 years of age of Alford, has provided the following information on the Memorial.

LANCASTER MEMORIAL ULCEBY CROSS

At midnight on 3rd March 1945 Geoff had completed a tour of duty at the Alford Royal Observer Corps post, code-named 'How Three' and returned home. He had only just arrived home when he heard the wailing sound of the siren, followed very closely by the sound of machine gun fire. Looking out of the bedroom window he saw that a Lancaster Mk III Bomber aircraft with four Rolls/Packard engines had been hit and was falling to the ground. The aircraft disappeared behind trees followed by a loud bang, indicating it had crashed.

Geoff then observed a German Nightfighter, a JU88-G, flying low over Alford in its endeavour to escape, this German aircraft was the cause of the Lancaster to crash.

Geoff also informed me that twenty-one aircraft were lost that night, due to German Nightfighters lurking in the skies over Lincolnshire waiting for returning aircraft from raids over Germany. However, the Lancaster that was shot down at Ulceby Cross had a new crew who was on a night training flight.

All seven crew died in the crash and note how young the four are who are buried in Alford Cemetery, their graves have the standard Commonwealth War Graves head stone. FO N A Ansdell, 21 years; FO A G Heath, 22 years; Sgt R O Parry, 19 years and Sgt A R Walker, 20 years. It is assumed the remaining three crew members would be in the same age group and it is understood they are buried in their respective home towns.

To mark the 50th Anniversary of this tragic crash, a memorial was erected in the gateway to the field in which the crew were killed and this is the inscription carved on the stone:

In the early hours of March 4th 1945
Lancaster PB 476 (PH 'Y')
No 12 Squadron RAF Wickenby
Crashed near this spot the victim of a
Luftwaffe intruder.
This memorial is placed here on the
50th Anniversary of the crash to
commemorate the crew who died.

Flying Officer N A Ansdell	Pilot
Flying Officer A Hunter	Navigator
Flying Officer A G Heath	Bomb Aimer
Sergeant R O Schafer	Flight Engineer
Sergeant R O Parry	Wireless Operator
Sergeant A R Walker	Mid Upper Gunner
Sergeant W Mellor	Rear Gunner

IN GRATEFUL REMEMBRANCE

Stanley Naylor, 2001

6th June 1944 is etched in our minds and Gillian Carter, Sunday Mirror 22nd May 1994, reminds us that it was a typical British Summer's Day - blustery, wet and overcast - but the greatest invasion force ever gathered couldn't wait for better weather. There was no turning back and the invasion proved to be a giant step on the road to victory.

LETHAL LADY

To watch her 'twix the goosenecks,
    On the flare path rolling fast;
Towards night sky with tail fins high,
    And a day's brief dusk long past.

Have you felt a hard stand tremble,
    To four Merlin's blasting roar?
And seen that tail wheel dancing
    To the slipstream's rushing bore?

Ever viewed a Lanc' on funnels,
    As she homed on a misty morn?
Maybe glimpsed her low on the downward leg,
    Heard her snarl at the breaking dawn?

Hell's Terror at night this Lady,
    As lethal still by day,
For her beauty concealed grim purpose,
    And the Lanc' had a debt to pay.

© *John R Walsh, 1985*

A BRIEF HISTORY OF THE SECOND WORLD WAR

Year 1939 September
Britain and France declared war on Germany on 3rd September 1939, following the German invasion of Poland on 1st September. In accordance with the Hitler Pact of August 1939, Russian troops also invaded Poland (and took back what was accepted by world leaders after 1st World War when Lord Curzon presided over international commission). Therefore the country was divided between the two invaders.

Phoney War October 1939 - April 1940
So-called because no significant military event affecting the Western Allies took place during the period. In January 1940, butter and bacon rationing were introduced in Britain.

German conquest of Western Europe, April 1940 - June 1940
Early in April 1940, the Germans overran Denmark, and went on to attack Norway, seeking control of Norwegian iron ore. The British sent a naval force to Narvik, but by June, Norway had surrendered and the British had suffered naval defeat. On the 10th May, the Germans invaded France, reaching the Channel ports and the outskirts of Dunkirk by the end of May.

Battle of Dunkirk, 27th May - 4th June 1940
200 naval ships and 600 small civilian craft evacuated 335,000 Allied troops from Dunkirk, leaving the bulk of their military equipment behind.

Fall of France, June 1940
Armistice signed between German and French Governments. Subsequent settlement set up nominally independent state under Marshall Petain, based on Vichy. The rest of France was directly occupied. General de Gaulle set up Free French in Britain.

Battle of Britain, July 1940 - September 1940
Air battle fought over Southern England by RAF Fighter Command and

German Luftwaffe. German object was to destroy possible air resistance to military invasion.

First Blitz, Winter 1940 - Spring 1941
RAF fighters near exhaustion, but, in early September, Germans switched tactics to night bombing of industrial cities; London, Coventry, Hull etc. 44,000 civilians were killed. Immense damage to buildings.

Other Fronts - War in North Africa
September 1940, Libyan based Italians invaded Egypt. British force counter-attacked, driving Italians back. Germans under General Rommel, reinforced Italians. British retreated, General Montgomery succeeded Wavell and, in October 1942, British forces won Battle of El Alamein. By May 1943 all North Africa was in Allied control.

War at Sea
After December 1939 (Battle of Plate), little threat from surface ships, but U-boats (submarines) in Atlantic nearly succeeded in starving Britain out. Eventually defeated by revised convoy system, with air support, and invention of radar.

War in Russia
In June 1941 Germans attacked Russia, having first secured control of Greece and Balkans. At first, German armies were immensely successful. Reached outskirts of Leningrad (Petersburg) and besieged city. Also reached outskirts of Moscow. Other German force drove through Ukraine. Russian answer was to move industries east and prepare counter attack, which came in December 1941. Battle of Stalingrad during winter of 1942 ended in January 1943 when German army surrendered with loss of 300,000 German soldiers.

Entry of USA - Pearl Harbour 1941
In December 1941, Japanese made surprise air attack on US Navy in Pearl Harbour, inflicting heavy losses. Hitler declared war on USA. Japanese successes continued. Invaded Malaysia. Singapore surrendered. Burma was also invaded, but Japanese failed to break through to India.

Western Allies regain Europe 1943 -1944

1) Italian campaign - very slow-moving and difficult. Mussolini was overthrown, but rescued by Germans and set as puppet ruler in Northern Italy. When Germans eventually retreated, Mussolini was captured by partisans and hanged.

2) D Day - June 6th 1944. US and British troops landed near Caen, using prefabricated harbour (Mulberry). Germans fought back but situation hopeless. Russians reached outskirts of Berlin. Hitler committed suicide. Germany surrendered 7th May 1945, ending War in Europe.

"Doodlebugs" - VS1 and VS2 rocket bombs

First VS1 offensive launched on London in June 1944, followed by VS2 offensive in September. VS1 and VS2 bombs were unmanned and operated automatically. VS2's were more deadly then VS1's. Much damage was done but, with victory already in sight, civilian morale was not seriously undermined.

Victory over Japan - Hiroshima and Nagasaki

Japanese were driven out of Burma by British, US made war in Pacific but gaining control of Pacific Islands was immensely costly in US lives. In August 1945 an atomic bomb dropped on Hiroshima (80,000 killed). A week later, a second atomic bomb was dropped on Nagasaki. On 14th August, Japan surrendered. The War was over.

Margaret Allen
(Reproduced from 'Civilians at War'
with permission of the publishers - Change Charity)

WARTIME - RECIPES

Almost immediately war was declared in September 1939 recipes appeared in the Boston Guardian newspaper that were cheap to make. Here are a sample of headings and recipes that appeared in the last four months of 1939.

'Salads for September Days'
'Nourishment in Time of Necessity'
'These Rabbit Dishes will make a Tasty Change'
'Serve Dishes that Save Expense'

COLOURFUL SALAD

This salad that is specially favoured because it looks as good as it tastes, and is a particularly nice accompaniment to cold meat, is best if arranged in oval dishes. The first outer layer is made of crisp lettuce leaves, light green in colour.

The centre is the rich crimson of beetroot, brought out by the addition of a little chopped dark green parsley and linking the crimson to the light green are segments of bright gold of ripe oranges.

The salad dressing should not be poured over the salad, but passed round individually.

VERY LIGHT LUNCH SALAD

This is excellent for children with bread and butter or toast and a glass of milk. It can equally be made into a decorated very light lunch salad. It requires dried carrots and potatoes, chopped parsley, shredded lettuce and slices of hard-boiled egg and it is topped with cream cheese. No attempt should be made at arranging this salad, but it should be served in a well-balanced jumble of colour.

SALAD SAUCE

This is the old-fashioned dressing, a little expensive and a little unusual, but then that is part of its delight. Take the yolks of two eggs, boiled hard, a dessertspoonful of grated Parmesan cheese, a little made mustard, a dessertspoonful of tarragon vinegar and a large tablespoonful of ketchup.

When well incorporated, add four dessertspoonfuls of salad oil and one dessertspoonful of vinegar. Beat so as to incorporate the oil with the other ingredients.

This mixture should not be poured on salads, but placed at the bottom of the bowl, to be stirred up when wanted. This method preserves the crispness of the lettuce. The quantity of the ingredients should be proportioned to the quantity of the salad and of course you can let each person dress his own salad if you serve in individual side dishes.

MAYONNAISE FOR SALAD

This too, is a good old-fashioned recipe which has stood the test of time. Put the yolk of an egg carefully freed from the white, into a basin and take away the speck. Beat the yolk lightly and add a pinch of salt and a pinch of pepper, pour some oil upon it, drop by drop at first and at the same time beat the sauce lightly and quickly. When it begins to thicken slightly increase the quantity of oil and continue beating until a thick, smooth, yellow paste.

Add gradually as much white wine vinegar as required according to your individual taste. The usually accepted as correct is about one teaspoonful of vinegar to eight of oil and the oil must be good and pure olive oil for mayonnaise.

Keep the mayonnaise in a cool place during the summer until wanted. You can add a little tarragon vinegar in making the sauce and it is generally preferred with this addition.

MIXED FRUIT SALAD

Candied peel, lemon or orange peel, lemon juice, any fruits in season, 3 oz. of sugar to each 1 lb. of fruit.

Prepare the fruit and remove pips if any. Place in a bowl, chop up very finely about a teaspoonful of lemon (or orange) peel to every pound of fruit and add, together with one teaspoonful of candid peel and a teaspoonful of lemon juice.

Sprinkle the sugar over all. Allow to stand for several hours, stirring frequently. If a very sharp fruit is used, it will be necessary to add a greater quantity of sugar.

ORANGE SALAD

Three oranges, 1 tablespoonful tarragon vinegar, pepper and salt, watercress, lettuce. Wash the cress and cut away the stalks. Drain well and arrange in a salad bowl. Peel the oranges and remove the pips. Cut into thin slices and place in the bowl. Mix all together well with a seasoning made of a tablespoonful each of tarragon vinegar and salad oil, add pepper and salt to taste. Arrange lettuce round the dish.

BARLEY BROTH

Take four ounces of pearl barley, two turnips and three ounces of maize meal. Wash the barley, steep for twelve hours, then put on the fire with five quarts of water. Add the turnips, chopped finely and boil for one hour, stir in the meal. Thin with more water if necessary and let it simmer gently for twenty minutes.

LENTIL SOUP

Allow one pint of lentils to two quarts of water. Pick over and wash the lentils and put them into a stewpan with the water. Bring slowly to the boil, skim clean and stew very gently for two hours, then add four leeks cut into long pieces (or two onions peeled and sliced), a carrot, washed and scraped, a small turnip, peeled, a half-a-dozen outer sticks of celery, or a sprig of parsley.

Let all stew gently for another two hours, skimming the soup occasionally as the scum rises to the surface. Strain the soup through a wire sieve into a basin, take out the parsley (if used) and rub all through the sieve into the basin. Return the soup to the stewpan and boil up again, stir in an ounce of margarine and dish up piping hot.

TURNIP SOUP

Peel a pound of turnips, cut into dice and chop two onions finely. Melt an ounce of margarine in a stewpot and throw in the vegetables, with a teaspoonful of brown sauce and a pint of stock or water. Simmer for half-an-hour or so, then moisten with milk and stir in half-a-teacupful of rice flour and as much milk as can be spared up to half-a-pint; boil all together for 20 minutes and serve.

HOT POT

Just right for busy days are nourishing hot pots. And try adding a little kidney. It imparts a savoury flavour to both beef and mutton. Trim and cut up 1lb lean mutton and ½lb sheeps' kidney and slice a few potatoes and two medium sized onions. Fry the meat lightly in a little dripping, then place in a casserole. Fry the potatoes and onions and add to the meat. Add one pint of stock, salt and pepper to taste, then put on the lid. Cook in a moderate oven for two hours. Thicken and serve piping hot.

SCOTCH EGGS

Ingredients: 4 hard-boiled eggs, ½lb sausage meat, 1 egg and breadcrumbs. Put the eggs into the boiling water and let the water cover them, then boil them gently for 15 minutes. Take them out and place them in a basin of cold water and when they are cold, shell them. Divide the sausage meat into four portions and cover each egg entirely with the sausage meat. Mould into the shape of a cork with flat ends. Roll them in a little flour, brush all over with a well-beaten egg, cover with breadcrumbs and fry a golden brown in very hot fat. The fat must cover them. Drain on paper, cut them in halves with a very sharp knife. Serve hot with potatoes or cold salad.

RABBIT PILAU

Prepare the rabbit and cut it up into 10 to 12 pieces. Rub each piece with a savoury mixture made by mixing the juice of two large onions with a teaspoonful of salt, half a teaspoonful of powdered ginger and the juice of a lemon. The onion juice may be obtained by bruising or grating the onions and draining off the liquor.

Boil a pound of rice in a quart of stock broth until it is half cooked. Whilst it is simmering melt four ounces of good fat in a saucepan and in it fry the pieces of rabbit until they are lightly browned, also two sliced onions. Put the meat into a deep earthen jar. Lay the onions upon it and cover with the rice. Add four cloves, eight peppercorns, a pinch of salt and a few strips of lemon rind and pour half a pint of milk over the whole. Fold paper over the top of the jar and bake in a moderate oven. If required add a little more broth or milk when the rabbit is half done. When the meat is sufficiently cooked pile the rice on a dish, place the pieces of meat on top and serve. Time required for baking, $1^1/_2$ to 2 hours.

SAVOURY RABBIT

Ingredients: 1 rabbit, 3 onions, a little sage, breadcrumbs, 1 oz butter, a good piece of dripping, salt and pepper.

Wash and joint the rabbit. Boil and chop the onions, add the crumbs, sage, seasoning and butter, mix well together. Melt the dripping in a baking tin, in this spread half the sage and onion stuffing. Arrange the rabbit joints, spread over the remainder of the stuffing and bake in a good oven.

PORK STEW

Ingredients: 1 lb spare rib of pork cut into chops, 2 spanish onions, 2 lb potatoes, 1 teaspoonful dried sage, salt and pepper.

Cut chops in half, slice onions. Peel potatoes and cut into rounds. Put a layer of pork in casserole. Cover with a layer of onions, half the sage and salt and pepper to taste. Next a layer of potatoes. Repeat layers until dish is full with a layer of potatoes on top. Half-fill the dishes with water cover with lid and cook 2 hours. Before quite cooked, remove lid and brown potatoes. Serve with apple sauce.

POTATO OMELETTE

Ingredients: 4 eggs, 1 tablespoonful milk, 1 oz butter, several small firm boiled potatoes.

Method: Break the eggs in a basin, beat them slowly until the whites mix with the yolks, add the milk and season with salt and pepper and a little grated nutmeg. Cut the potatoes into rings and keep them to hand. Melt the butter in a pan until it turns slightly golden brown and pour in the eggs. Stir slowly with a fork, adding the sliced potatoes as you stir till the eggs just begin to set, then tip the pan, shape the omelette neatly and roll it. Hold it over the gas for a minute and serve immediately on a really hot plate.

BACON SAVOURY

The end of a piece of boiled bacon makes an appetising 'toastie'. Melt a nut of butter in a pan, add a teaspoonful of boiled rice, 3 ozs minced cold boiled bacon, two tablespoonsfuls of tomato ketchup and a quarter of a pint of stock. Simmer exactly for 20 minutes, stirring occasionally to prevent burning. Then serve on rounds of buttered toast or fried bread.

BREAD PUDDING

A good way of using up the leftover bread and butter. The children will love the pineapple flavour. Arrange the slices of stale bread and butter in neat strips in a buttered pie-dish, sprinkling each layer with sugar and fruit. The pineapple should be shredded or crushed. Add some salt to $1/2$ pint of milk. Heat and pour it on to a beaten egg. Strain into the pie-dish, grate a little nutmeg on the top and soak for half-an-hour. Decorate the top of the pudding with shredded pineapple.

TREACLE TART

Line a plate with pastry. Mix 4 tablespoonfuls treacle with 2 of water, then stir in 6 large tablespoonfuls bread crumbs. Add the grated rind of an orange. Spread the pastry with this, then sprinkle a few currants on the top. Now put on top of pastry and bake for 15 minutes in a hot oven. Instead of currants, a few slices of apple is a nice addition.

SODA CAKE

1 lb flour, $1/4$ lb butter or lard, $1/4$ lb margarine, $1/2$ lb sugar, $1/2$ lb currants, grated lemon rind, 2 eggs, $1/4$ pint boiling milk, grated nutmeg, 1 teaspoonful bicarbonate soda. Rub the lard and margarine into the flour, rub the sugar over a lemon rind. Mix all the dry ingredients. Make a well in the middle. Put in the warm milk and soda, add the eggs and use water or tea to make a good cake mixing. Bake $1\,1/2$ hours in a moderate oven.

SPONGE PUDDING

Put an apple in a deep pie-dish, strew with sugar. Beat $1/4$ lb margarine,

¼ lb sugar and one egg, then mix in ½ self-raising flour. You will need a little milk to put over the apples, bake until firm and light brown.

'BULLY BEEF'

'Bully Beef' is not such a 'course' stand-by as most people imagine and it is easy to make appetising-potted meat from a quarter-pound of this.

Run it twice through a mincer, add a little grated nutmeg and pepper to taste. Dissolve a quarter of a meat cube in a tablespoonful of water and mix it with the meat, then mash thoroughly with a wooden spoon. When smooth, press it into a small glass dish, cover with melted margarine or dripping. The children will relish it more in their sandwiches when 'done-up' in this fashion.

('Bully beef was consistantly used in France and Germany in 1944/45. One cook found two or three different ways of serving this mundane meat. The one that turned out to be tasty was cutting the 'bully beef' (often referred to as corn beef) into slices and dipped them in batter, then cooking them the same as 'fish and chips'. This made a very tasty dish!) S.N.

A SAVOURY PUDDING

Here again 'bully beef' is used. You require half-a-pound of beef, 3 ounces of shredded suet, one large onion, a teaspoonful of oatmeal, a cupful of stock and a teaspoonful of meat extract dissolved in a teacupful of water. Chop the 'bully beef' finely, also chop the onion and mix well with the suet. Toast the oatmeal until crisp, add it and season well. Pour into a greased basin and steam for two hours.

The paper states: 'Don't throw away cold potatoes, use them as follows'.

PLAIN SCONES

Peel a pound of cold potatoes boiled in their skins, mash them, then warm two tablespoonfuls of milk and add it with an ounce of margarine and a pinch of salt. Mix in about a quarter-pound of flour and when a nice paste is formed, roll it out very thinly. Cut it into rounds, place them on a hot flowered gridle, cook for three minutes on one side, then turn over and cook three minutes on the other side.

CURRANT SCONES

To make sweet scones you need the same quantity of potatoes as for plain scones, also two ounces of dripping or lard, $1/2$ lb of flour and an ounce each of sugar and currants. Cream the fat with the sugar, rub into the flour, then mash the potatoes and add them to the mixture with the currants and a pinch of salt. Mix with just enough milk to moisten and when a fairly firm paste is formed, roll out, cut into scone shapes and bake in a good oven for half-an-hour.

POTATO DOUGHNUTS

Pass some cold beef through a mincer and mix it with half the quantity of breadcrumbs. Add pepper and salt to season, also a little chopped onion and use half-an-egg to blend. Mash some freshly boiled potatoes well and mix with the other half of the egg. Form the meat into small balls, dip them in flour and coat each one with the mashed potatoes. Dip into egg and breadcrumbs and fry in plenty of boiling fat until nicely browned.

POTATO BREAD

Take equal quantities of flour and mashed potatoes, also yeast, salt and water. Boil in their skins as many potatoes as are required, cooking until quite soft. Remove the skins, weigh the potatoes, then mash or beat them to pulp. Add to the flour and salt, rub well together and add yeast. Knead well, adding as much water as is necessary to make the mixture sufficiently solid, yet light. Form into loaves and place in the oven, which should be only moderately hot, if very hot, it will make the outsides of the loaves very hard, as potato bread requires longer and slower baking then ordinary bread. Leave the door open for a few minutes after the loaves are first put in.

SOUR MILK SCONES

Sour milk makes excellent scones as follows: Mix 6 ozs of flour, 1 oz of sugar, two tablespoons sultanas, one tablespoonful currants, $1/2$ teaspoonful of cream of tartar and a pinch of salt. Rub in 2 ozs butter, then add the yolk of an egg and sufficient sour milk to form a smooth stiff paste. Fold in the white of an egg, then fill some small greased patty tins with the mixture. Brush over with beaten egg and bake in a fairly quick oven. Split open and spread with butter.

WALNUT BREAD

1 cup chopped walnuts, 1 cup caster sugar, 4 cups flour, 1 teaspoonful salt, 2 cups milk, 1 egg, 4 teaspoonfuls baking powder. Sift flour, salt and baking powder into basin. Add sugar. Dilute egg with milk and stir into the flour, then add chopped walnuts and stir well. Place in two buttered loaf tins. Stand 20 minutes in a warm place. Bake $1/2$ an hour or until ready in a moderate oven. Keep at least one day before cutting.

SAVOURY ONION CUSTARD

Ingredients: 1 oz butter, $1 3/4$ lbs onions, 2 eggs, $1/2$ pint milk, seasoning. Melt the butter in a frying pan and put in the sliced onion. Sauté for about 12 minutes, tossing and stirring frequently. Turn into a greased casserole. Beat the eggs with the milk and plenty of seasoning. Pour over the onion. Put into a slow oven and bake for 30 minutes or until set.

POTATO CAKES

Take $1/2$ lb cooked potatoes, 1 oz lard, 1 oz sugar, 4 ozs flour, one teaspoonful of baking powder. Mash the potatoes. Mix in the fat, sugar, flour and baking powder. Work into a paste. Roll out and cut into rounds. Fry in boiling fat until a golden brown on either side. Drain on kitchen paper. Butter and serve hot.

Produced from the Boston Guardian 1939
by permission of The British Library

The bottom photograph on the front cover and the following four photographs have been reproduced by kind permission of the Island History Trust, Dockland Settlement, 197 East Ferry Road, London, E14 3BA. The photographs may not be reproduced in any form without prior written permission of the Trust.

READY FOR THE BLITZ at Millwall Central School, East London.
Reproduction by kind permission of Island History Trust

AUXILLIARY WAR WORKERS at Isle of Dogs Baths, East London, 1940.
Reproduction by kind permission of Island History Trust

SECOND WORLD WAR BOMB DAMAGE, Millwall Central, East London.
Reproduction by kind permission of Island History Trust

WAR-TIME EVACUEES from Millwall, East London, 1940 or 1942.

Reproduction by kind permission of Island History Trust

Aerial photo of the Great Northern Hotel, centre of photo, demolished to make way for Pell's Drive, see next photo.
Photo loaned by Colin Cumberworth.

Entrance to Pell's Drive, site of Great Northern Hotel. Approximate position of snipers platform in the tree partly obscured on the extreme left of photo.
Photo Colin Cumberworth.

'B' Company Kirton Home Guard. My father, Fred Naylor, second from the right in the front row standing. Photo loaned by kind permission of Norman Grey, 88 years of age, 6th from the right in the front row standing.

Glancey's bag and flying jacket on display at
the 388th Collection, Market Western.
*Produced by permission of the curator, David Sarson.
Photo Stanley Naylor, 2001*

United States Air Force Boeing B-17 Fortress.
Produced by permission of David Sarson

Beaufighter Aircraft.
Photo Merlins, Fourways, East Kirkby.

USAAF uniforms meticulously displayed at the 388th Collection,
Hillside Fam, Market Western.
Photo David Sarson, curator.

155

Fully restored control tower at Lincolnshire Aviation Heritage Centre.
Produced by permission of the Heritage Centre
Photo Stanley Naylor, 2001

Women's Land Army marching through Wisbech during
Peace Celebrations 1945.
Photo by permission of Lillian Ream Trust

Typical concrete wartime pillbox.
Photo Stanley Naylor, 2000

Lancaster Bomber NX611 'Just Jane' and David Brown
Tug Tractor towing Bomb Carrier.
Photo Phillip Panton
By courtesy of Lincolnshire Aviation Heritage Centre East Kirkby

The bare ground where Hagnaby 'Dummy Airfield' was sited.
Photo Stanley Naylor, 2001

Typical concrete wartime pill box, gun emplacement or observation post.
Photo Stanley Naylor, 2001

Group of Civil Defence, Long Sutton 1945.
Photo by permission of Lillian Ream Trust

Photo by permission of Lillian Ream Trust

Group of police from Sutton Bridge, 1944.
Photo by permission of Lillian Ream Trust

Sutton St Edmunds Home Guard, 1941.
Photo by permission of Lillian Ream Trust

Italian POW's riddling potatoes, 1944.
Photo by permission of Lillian Ream Trust

A farming scene - heaps of sugar beet after being topped.
Photo by permission of Lillian Ream Trust

A farming scene - picking late potatoes.
Photo by permission of Lillian Ream Trust

Headstone near Ulceby Cross, in memory of seven air-crew who
were killed when their Lancaster crashed close to this site.
Photo Stanley Naylor, 2001

Memorial in the middle of a field where five Lancaster aircrew are buried.
Photo Stanley Naylor

Hants and Dorset No. 2594 Grimsby Dock Basin 1943.
Photo Mrs J Miller via Graham Chaters

High Speed Launch 63' Whaleback No. 142 Grimsby Dock Basin 1940.
Photo Leo Chapman via Graham Chaters

Searchlight similar to the one that arrived in Kirton Skeldyke in September 1939.
*Photo Stanley Naylor. Produced by permission of Mr Houldershaw
Allied Forces Military Museum, Stickford*

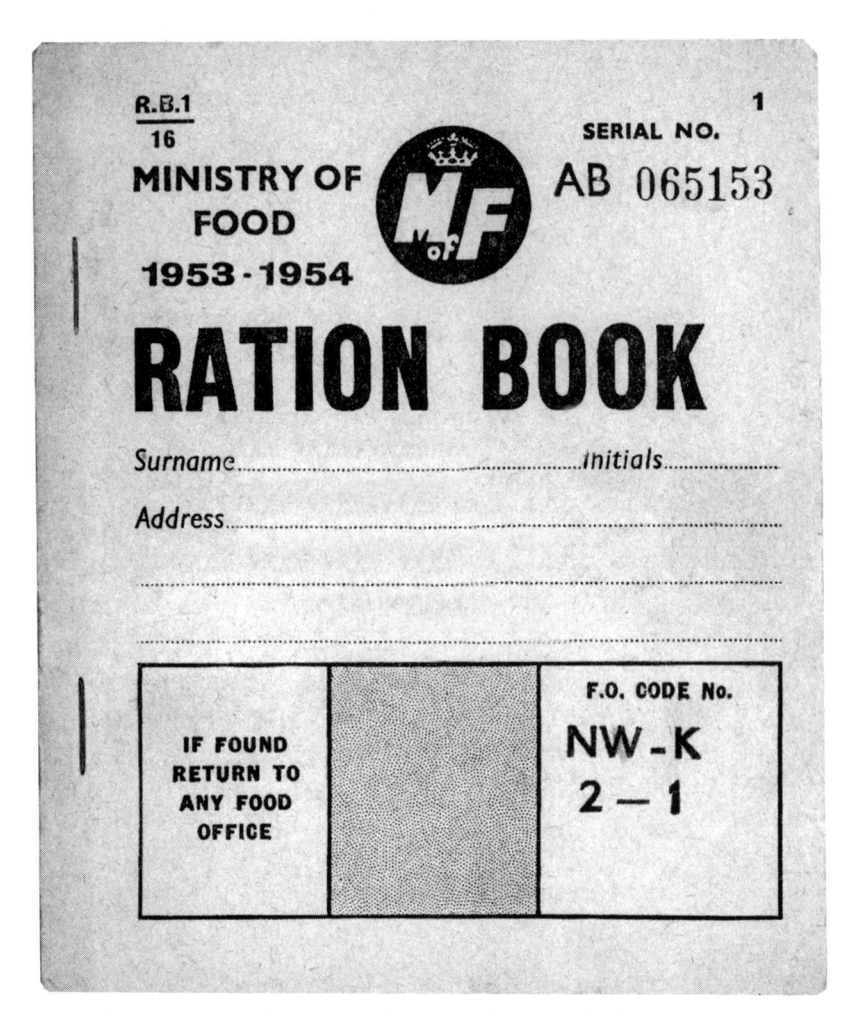

As you see by the date on this ration book, rationing continued after the war and finally ended in June 1954.

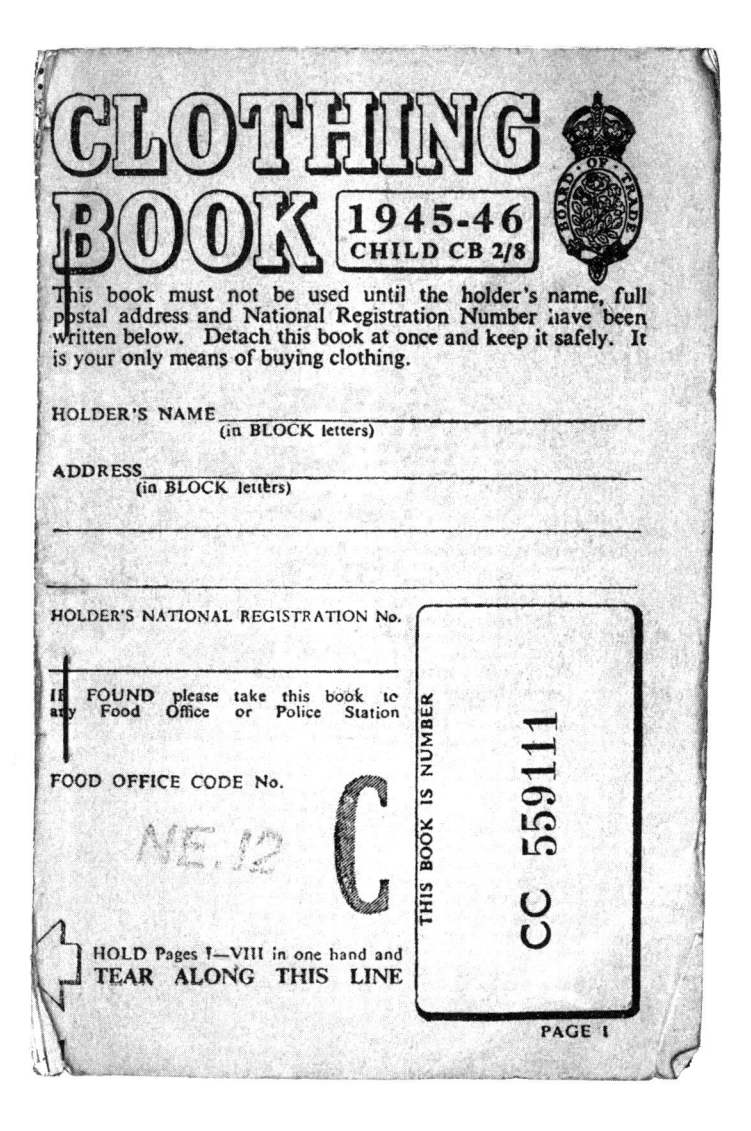

CLOTHING BOOK 1945-46
CHILD CB 2/8

This book must not be used until the holder's name, full postal address and National Registration Number have been written below. Detach this book at once and keep it safely. It is your only means of buying clothing.

HOLDER'S NAME _____
(in BLOCK letters)

ADDRESS _____
(in BLOCK letters)

_____

_____

HOLDER'S NATIONAL REGISTRATION No. _____

IF FOUND please take this book to any Food Office or Police Station

FOOD OFFICE CODE No.

NE.12

C

THIS BOOK IS NUMBER **CC 559111**

HOLD Pages I—VIII in one hand and **TEAR ALONG THIS LINE**

NATIONAL REGISTRATION IDENTITY CARD

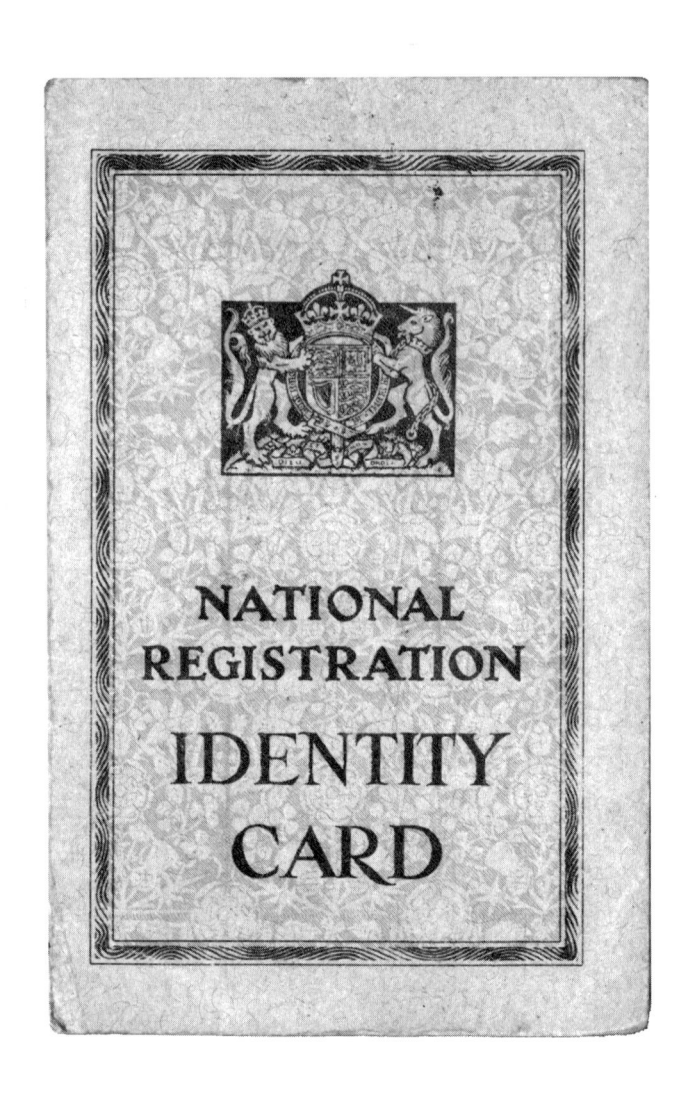

MINISTRY OF FOOD

REASONS FOR RATIONING

War has meant the re-planning of our food supplies. Half our meat and most of our bacon, butter and sugar come from overseas. Here are four reasons for rationing :—

① RATIONING PREVENTS WASTE OF FOOD We must not ask our sailors to bring us unnecessary food cargoes at the risk of their lives.

② RATIONING INCREASES OUR WAR EFFORT Our shipping carries food, and armaments in their raw and finished state, and other essential raw materials for home consumption and the export trade. To reduce our purchases of food abroad is to release ships for bringing us other imports. So we shall strengthen our war effort.

③ RATIONING DIVIDES SUPPLIES EQUALLY There will be ample supplies for our 44½ million people, but we must divide them fairly, everyone being treated alike. No one must be left out.

④ RATIONING PREVENTS UNCERTAINTY Your Ration Book assures you of your fair share. Rationing means that there will be no uncertainty — *and no queues*.

YOUR RATION BOOK IS YOUR PASSPORT TO EASY PURCHASING OF BACON & HAM, BUTTER AND SUGAR

AN ANNOUNCEMENT BY THE MINISTRY OF FOOD, GT. WESTMINSTER HOUSE. LONDON. S.W.1

FOOD MF FACTS

The new Ration Book:
RE-REGISTER
as soon as you get yours

When you get your new Ration Book write your address on the front cover, and your name, address and National Registration Number on the front of the Clothing Book which is bound inside it. Remove the Clothing Book carefully and put it away in a safe place until the time comes to use it.

After this you must register afresh with all your retailers (except for milk) even if you wish to remain with your present retailers, as most people will. You cannot re-register for milk.

HOW TO RE-REGISTER

(1) On page 5 of the Ration Book, write your name, National Registration Number and address in Section A, and at the top of page 6, your *present* milk retailer's name and address.

(2) In the other spaces on page 6, write the names and addresses of the retailers with whom you wish to register. (If you know that your retailer uses a rubber stamp, you can leave this job to him.)

(3) On page 8, write your name and address in the spaces against MEAT, EGGS (if you buy them from a retailer), FATS, CHEESE, BACON, SUGAR.

(4) Take the Ration Book to each retailer to cut out the proper counterfoils. *Don't cut them out yourself.*

IMPORTANT—Re-register as soon as you get your new Ration Book. But if you are moving house before July 22nd, wait to re-register in your new area.

HOLIDAY SWEETS & CHOCOLATES
Although you may be able to buy sweets when you are away on holiday, if you are wise you will get them before you leave home.

ORANGE JUICE FOR "UP TO 10's"
DON'T MISS YOUR CHANCE!
The temporary increase in orange juice supplies has made it possible to extend the allocation during May and June to include children from 5 to 10 years old. Don't miss this chance of giving extra Vitamin C to your child. A bottle of orange juice lasting a fortnight costs 5d. Take the blue ration book and 5d. *in stamps* to your nearest distribution centre or Food Office.

The Ministry of Food, London, W.1   Food Facts No. 256

Thank you, Mrs. Ruggles... we want more like you!

Mrs. Ruggles keeps the little sweet and cigarette shop in the village. She's been looking after her "evacuee" for over six months. Extra work? Yes, Johnnie's been a handful! .... but she knows she has done the right thing.

And think of all the people who have cause to be thanking Mrs. Ruggles. First, young Johnnie himself. He's out of a danger zone—where desperate peril may come at any minute. And he's healthier and happier and better-behaved now. Perhaps he doesn't say it but he certainly means "Thank you, Mrs. Ruggles". Then his parents. Think what it means to them! "Whatever happens Johnnie is safe. And with such a dear motherly soul, too. We often say 'Bless you, Mrs. Ruggles'."

The Government too is grateful to Mrs. Ruggles—and to all the 300,000 others who are looking after evacuated children. But many new volunteers are needed—to share the present burden, and to prepare for any crisis that may come. Won't you be one of them? You may be saving another Johnnie's life.

The Minister of Health, who has been entrusted by the Government with the conduct of evacuation, asks you urgently to join the Roll of those who are willing to receive children. Please apply to your local Council.

FOOD FACTS
Number 27

THANKS to the hard work of our farmers and growers, there are fine supplies of potatoes, carrots and oatmeal in the Country. Three foods giving energy and protection against illness — let us eat some of each every day.

The crews of our mine-sweepers are always risking their lives to bring you food, so don't waste any. You wouldn't if you'd done any sweeping yourself!

ON THE KITCHEN FRONT

Potato Carrot Pancake

Well-seasoned mashed potato combined with cooked carrot makes a wholesome and savoury-tasting pancake. Whip the mashed potato to a loose creamy consistency. Season well with pepper and salt and add some diced cooked carrot. Pan-fried slowly in a very little fat it develops a deliciously crisp crust, but it can be baked to a good brown in the oven if preferred.

Potato Basket

Scrub 1 lb. potatoes and boil gently in a very little water. When they are nearly cooked, drain off the liquid reserving it for stock. Let them finish cooking in their own steam by covering them closely with a folded cloth under the lid and standing the saucepan at the side of the stove until they are floury. Peel and mash well. Add a beaten egg and mash again. Grease a cake tin and coat it with browned breadcrumbs. Press in the mashed potatoes to form a thick lining to the tin. Bake in a hot oven for about 10 minutes. Meanwhile dice 1 lb. carrots, having cooked them for 15 minutes, and mix them with a sauce made from 1 oz. dripping, 1 oz. oatmeal and ½ pint milk or stock, and salt and pepper to taste. When the potato basket is cooked, turn it out and fill it with the hot carrot mixture. Heat in the oven for a few minutes and serve piping hot. (*Enough for four*.)

You can hear all kinds of food tips on the wireless at 8.15 every morning

Oatmeal Stuffing

This is particularly useful for making meat, fish or poultry go further.

Boil 3 ozs. coarse oatmeal in 1½ teacupfuls water for 30 minutes. Mix well with 2 ozs. breadcrumbs, salt and pepper, 1 teaspoonful mixed sweet herbs, 1 teaspoonful chopped parsley, 1 grated onion (if you can get it) and a pinch of mace if liked. Bind with a little melted dripping if necessary.

Do you know?

1. That over-cooking meat not only spoils the flavour but makes it shrink too.
2. That by grating vegetables a good soup can be made in 20 minutes.

THE MINISTRY OF FOOD, LONDON, S.W.1

YORKSHIRE PUDDING
(without baking powder)

Time: Preparation 10 minutes. Cooking 20-30 minutes. *Ingredients:* 4 oz. wheatmeal flour, ½ teaspoonful salt, ½ pint milk. *Quantity:* 4 helpings. *Method:* Mix flour and salt, make a well in the middle and pour in a third of the milk, beat well, add rest of milk, stand for an hour and pour into a tin containing smoking hot dripping. Bake in a hot oven (450° F. or Regulo 7) for 20-30 minutes.

WHEATMEAL SCONES

Time: Preparation 5 minutes. Cooking 10 minutes. *Ingredients:* 4 oz. wheatmeal flour, 4 oz. mashed, cooked potato, 1 oz. fat, ¼ teaspoonful of salt, 1 oz. sultanas or currants, 1 small teacupful 'household' milk. *Quantity:* 12-16 scones. *Method:* Mix flour and salt. Rub fat into flour, add mashed potato, mix into a soft dough with the milk. Roll out to ¼ in. thickness, cut into rounds. Cook in a hot oven for 10 minutes.

POTATO PASTRY

Time: Preparation 6 minutes. Cooking 30 minutes. *Ingredients:* 8 oz. wheatmeal flour, 4 oz. mashed cooked potato, 2 oz. fat, ½ teaspoonful salt, 2 tablespoonfuls water. *Quantity:* 4-6 helpings. *Method:* Cream fat and potatoes, work in flour, salt, and water to form a stiff paste. Use for pastry cases, flans, pie coverings, etc.

THIS WEEK'S FOOD FACTS

The plus bread

Apart from its benefit to our health, National Wheatmeal Bread will save many thousands of tons of shipping. But our stocks of white flour must not be wasted. So the change from white bread to National Wheatmeal will be gradual. Until white flour is exhausted, bakers may use up to one-quarter of white flour in making National Wheatmeal Bread. *After April 6th* there will be no more white bread, but up to one-quarter white flour may, for a time, still go into National Wheatmeal. *After April 20th* cakes, buns, biscuits, etc., must contain not less than three-quarters Wheatmeal. For home baking, white flour may be bought until retailers' stocks are used up. Speciality brown breads will still be permitted under licence.

You'll like National Wheatmeal Flour for cooking. Here are two tips on how to get the best results when making cakes, etc :—
1. National Wheatmeal Flour needs a little more moisture when mixed for cakes, pastry, bread. A fairly soft consistency bakes best.
2. National Wheatmeal Flour needs more salt, less sugar, less suet.

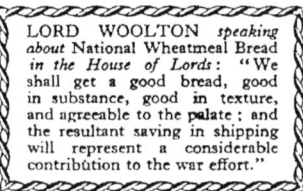

> LORD WOOLTON *speaking about* National Wheatmeal Bread *in the House of Lords*: "We shall get a good bread, good in substance, good in texture, and agreeable to the palate; and the resultant saving in shipping will represent a considerable contribution to the war effort."

*Food obtained
By methods shifty
Is shared with Hitler
Fifty-fifty.*

FOOD FACTS No. 89

Poz. on that Oz.!

We don't want to stint either ourselves or our families, but we mustn't waste an ounce of bread. If every one of us could save a slice of bread each day — just one ounce — we should save 4,500 tons of shipping in a year, and who knows how many precious lives; so it isn't enough to be just bread-conscious; we must become crust-conscious — yes, even crumb-conscious.

SAVE BREAD by—Allowing new bread to become quite cold before putting it into the bread bin : Using bread when it is 24 hours old, and never when it is new because you get more slices to the loaf : Using stale bread for browned breadcrumbs, rusks for children, bread puddings, sweet or savoury, for thickening soups, as breakfast cereal, or (soaked in water and squeezed out) for stuffing : By keeping it in a clean, dry bin swathed in a clean cloth : By not eating it at the same meal as potatoes.

FOOD FACTS
Our CHRISTMAS Rations

There will be special rations of sugar, butter and margarine, meat, and sweets. Vegetarians will be able to get extra cheese instead of meat. The following are the Christmas rations for all holders of the General Buff Ration Book (R.B.1), Child's Green Book (R.B.2), Junior Blue Book (R.B.4), and Ration Cards R.B.8R and R.B.8X.

Sugar
The sugar coupon No. 22 will be worth 1½ lb. sugar — instead of ½ lb. normal ration. This coupon can be used at any time during the four-week period No. 6 (Dec. 9-Jan. 5).

Butter and Margarine
The fats coupon No. 22 will be worth 12 oz. butter and margarine (not more than 6 oz. butter) and 2 oz. cooking fats (instead of the normal ration 6 oz. butter and margarine, and 2 oz. cooking fats). This coupon can be used at any time during four-week period No. 6 (Dec. 9-Jan. 5).

Meat
Increased from 1/2 to 2/- (7d. to 1/- for children — R.B.2 holders). The amount of meat available on each coupon (two in R.B.1 and R.B.4, one in R.B.2) for week No. 22 (Scotland, week 23) will be 1/- of which about 3d. worth will be canned corned meat. On Form R.G.48 the value of each extra meat ration will be 2/- (Child 1/-). This coupon No. 22, Dec. 16-Dec. 22 (in Scotland, No. 23, Dec. 23-Dec. 29), can be used *only during that week*.

FOR VEGETARIANS authorised on Form R.G.48 to obtain the special cheese ration, the cheese coupon for week No. 22 (Scotland, week 23) will be worth 18 oz. (36 oz. where two special rations are authorised); the coupon can be used at any time during four-week period No. 6 (Dec. 9-Jan. 5).

SPECIAL CASES
TEMPORARY RATION CARD R.B.12. The increased rations may be obtained against Form R.B.12 valid in week No. 22 (Scotland, week 23) unless already taken against coupons in a ration book. WEEKLY SEAMAN'S RATION BOOK R.B.6 and DUTY RATION CARD R.B.8A. Additional Christmas rations will not be obtainable on the fats, sugar and meat coupons in these books or cards.

Chocolates and Sweets
The arrangements for obtaining the extra 4 oz. of chocolate and sweets will be given in *Food Facts* in Sunday and daily newspapers between Dec. 9 and 15.

MORE FOOD FACTS BY RADIO AT 8.20 A.M. ON THURSDAY.

THE MINISTRY OF FOOD, LONDON, W.1.   FOOD FACTS No. 28.

MINISTRY OF FOOD

MEAT RATIONING

Meat is now rationed—the full ration is 1/10d. worth per week, or 11d. for young children with a Child's Ration Book.

Meat Coupon No. 10 is valid for this week, No. 11 for next week, and so on. Coupons Nos. 1 to 9 are therefore not required, and should be cut out and destroyed.

No coupons are required for liver, kidney, tripe, heart, ox-tail, etc., or for poultry or game. Sausages, meat pies and galantines containing not more than 50% meat are not to be rationed at present.

No coupons are required for meat served by Canteens, Schools, Restaurants and Catering Establishments — which are all rationed at the sources of supply.

WHEN SHOPPING REMEMBER:

1 During the war our meat supplies are bound to vary from time to time. When you cannot get just what you want in a particular week, be ready to take something else — your butcher will be glad to advise you.

2 When you cannot get imported beef, bear in mind that our Fighting Forces, whose needs must come first, consume a large proportion of our supplies. Remember that the eating of home-killed instead of imported meat saves shipping space and foreign exchange.

RATIONING IS PART OF NATIONAL DEFENCE

AN ANNOUNCEMENT BY THE MINISTRY OF FOOD, GT. WESTMINSTER HOUSE, LONDON, S.W.1

Now comes Part 5 in the POTATO PLAN

Use Potatoes in place of flour

(PART POTATOES, PART FLOUR)

Have you tried this latest addition to the Potato Plan? Here it is :
Use potatoes in place of part of the flour, when making pastry, puddings and cakes. The potatoes can be cooked the day before, if more convenient, and mashed while hot. Watch out for further recipes in this series.

POTATO PASTRY

Rubbing-in method. 4 ozs. mashed potatoes ; 8 ozs. flour ; 2 ozs. fat; ¼ teaspoonful salt. Mix flour and salt, rub in fat, then work into the potato. Mix to a stiff dough, with a small amount of cold water if necessary. Knead and roll out.

Creaming method. 4 ozs. mashed potatoes ; 8 ozs. flour ; 2 ozs. fat ; ¼ teaspoonful salt. Cream fat and potato, add the flour and salt. No moisture is necessary. Mix to a stiff dough and roll out.

The 4 other parts of the Plan

1 Serve potatoes for breakfast on three days a week.

2 Make your main dish potato dish one day a week.

3 Refuse second helpings of other food. Have more potatoes instead.

4 Serve potatoes in other ways than "plain boiled."

**Bread costs ships . . .
Eat home-grown potatoes instead**

ISSUED BY THE MINISTRY OF FOOD, LONDON, W.I.
P.22.

BOSTON CO-OPERATIVE SOCIETY, Ltd.

FOOD RATION SCHEME

YOU ARE INVITED TO REGISTER WITH THE SOCIETY FOR—

BACON and HAM BUTTER-SUGAR

We have the assurance from the Ministry of Food that WE SHALL RECEIVE FULL SUPPLIES TO MEET ALL INDIVIDUAL REQUIREMENTS.

It is open to any holder of a Ration Book to register forthwith

CO-OP

REGISTER AT ANY GROCERY BRANCH

FULL DIVIDEND
will be allowed
TO MEMBERS ON
ALL PURCHASES
including
RATIONED FOODS

Holland War Agricultural Executive Committee

8th July, 1940.

Urgent Notice to All Farmers

In response to an urgent appeal by the Prime Minister, the Committee has undertaken, in collaboration with the Army and R.A.F. Authorities, to arrange for the immediate provision of obstructions against the landing of enemy aircraft in all fields, throughout the Holland Division, which allow a clear run of 250 yards or more in any direction.

At this moment of grave National emergency the Committee earnestly appeals to farmers and farm workers to proceed with this work AT ONCE, and it is hoped that farm workers will assist with voluntary labour after working hours.

The matter is of urgent and vital necessity, demanding the utmost energy and speed on the part of the whole farming community, to whom the Committee looks for a display of commonsense and patriotism, and a total disregard of any personal loss or inconvenience that may be involved. Upon the action taken within the next few hours may depend the fate, not only of the land and crops, but of the whole country.

Farmers should communicate by telephone IMMEDIATELY with the Executive Officer, County Hall, Boston (Tel. 3313), or with the Chairman of the District Sub-Committee in their area, by whom directions will be given as to the measures to be taken.

THERE IS NOT A MOMENT TO LOSE

KESTEVEN WAR AGRICULTURAL EXECUTIVE COMMITTEE.

FARMERS REQUIRING ADDITIONAL LABOUR

for corn harvest, potato picking and beet lifting are earnestly urged to apply at once to their Local Labour Exchange, or to the undersigned, without delay.

The following classes of supplementary labour may be available:—

- Women's Land Army (both permanent and seasonal workers).
- University Students (18/24).
- Secondary school boys and girls (15/18).
- Belgian, Dutch and Norwegian refugees with experience of land work.

Failure to apply NOW may mean that the labour will not be available when required.

ALAN L SMALL,
County Executive Officer.

County Offices,
SLEAFORD.

TO
EMPLOYEES
AND
EMPLOYERS

A Method of Week-by-Week Saving to help Win the War

TO EMPLOYEES

Save together and save regularly—to help your Country in the fight for freedom. By joining the National Savings Group in your factory or office you will find it easier to save regularly and in small sums. If there is no Savings Group at your place of employment set about forming one.

TO EMPLOYERS

Help your employees to form a National Savings Group at your factory or office. The National Savings Committee has schemes designed to meet every need; they are an easy to organise and simple to work. There is a scheme to suit your requirements. By making it easy for your employees to save regularly on pay day you will be helping them to make their contribution to the nation's financial effort.

WRITE TO THE NATIONAL SAVINGS COMMITTEE, LONDON, S.W.1 WHO WILL GIVE YOU EVERY PRACTICAL ASSISTANCE IN FORMING YOUR NATIONAL SAVINGS GROUP

AND TO EVERY BRITISH CITIZEN

If you cannot join a National Savings Group you can still save in small sums by purchasing 6d. National Savings Stamps at any Post Office. It is a simple way to save, and since your savings are to-day a vital contribution to victory make a point of putting some away every week.

LEND TO DEFEND
THE RIGHT TO BE FREE

ISSUED BY THE NATIONAL SAVINGS COMMITTEE

FOR BRIGHTER DARKER EVENINGS—

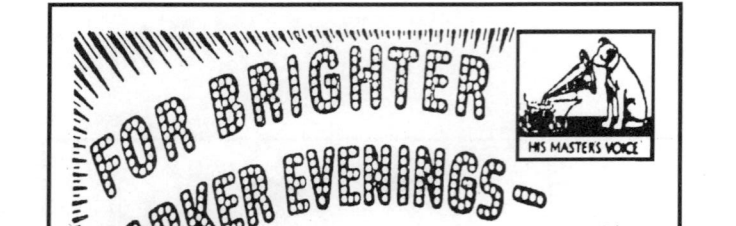

you need "HIS MASTER'S VOICE" RADIO

Model No. 1102

● 5-valve A.C. superhet receiver. Three waveband. Eight station push-buttons. Fluid light tuning. 15½ Gns. or by Hire Purchase.

In your home. We recommend it for the trustworthy quality of its components, for its unrivalled tonal purity, its sound performance, And it costs no more than ordinary radio. May we demonstrate, and quote easy terms?

DEMONSTRATIONS IN YOUR HOME OR IN OUR SHOWROOMS.

HURST, SON & PAGE Ltd.
16, MARKET PLACE, BOSTON

HOLLAND COUNTY COUNCIL
AIR RAID PRECAUTIONS

DUMPING OF SUGAR BEET ON ROADSIDES.

The County Council hereby give notice that all Farmers and Sugar Beet Growers must refrain from dumping sugar beet on the roadsides in the County, in the interests of Public Safety.

The County Council hope all Growers will co-operate with them in this important matter.

H. C. MARRIS,
A.R.P. Controller.

8th September, 1939.

Holland War Agricultural Executive Committee

FARM SUNDAY

His Worship The Mayor of Boston
(Coun. G. H. Bird, J.P.)

will preside at a

MASS DEMONSTRATION

to be held in the

Central Park Boston,
on Sunday, 4th July, 1943

PROGRAMME

2.45 to 3. Local Contingents and Bodies representative of every sphere of local life and work will assemble on the parade ground in the Central Park.

3.15 SHORT RELIGIOUS SERVICE.
A Massed Choir will lead the singing of the Hymns and the officiating clergy will be Canon A. M. Cook, M.A. (Vicar of Boston) & the Rev. R. Fleneley (representing the Free Churches)

3.30 Speaker: Major R. G. Proby, M.C., the Minister of Agriculture's Liaison Officer.

3.45 The **Rt. Hon. R. S. HUDSON, M.P.**, Minister of Agriculture and Fisheries, whose speech will be broadcast by the B.B.C. from a similar demonstration at Ormskirk, Lancashire. Following the Minister's Address, Mr. H. W. Butcher, M P. will move an important resolution.

Proceedings will terminate with a march past.

Everybody Interested in Agriculture & in the Welfare of the Nation during the coming struggle should make every effort to attend this important function.

HOLLAND WAR AGRICULTURAL EXECUTIVE COMMITTEE.

PIECE WORK RATES FOR 1943.

A CONFERENCE between representatives of the National Farmers' Union and the National Union of Agricultural Workers in the South Holland area was held at Spalding on Saturday, March 27th, 1943. The prices to be paid for work done during 1943 were agreed in principle and a Committee was elected to draft an agreement and publish the prices. The Committee met on Saturday, April 10th and the following agreement was reached.

That the district be divided into two areas known as District No. 1 and District No. 2.

District No. 1 to be the seaward side of the main road running from Donington, through Spalding to Cowbit and thence on to the South Holland Drain and to include the villages of Donington Quadring Gosberton Surfleet and Pinchbeck and the town of Spalding. To the North of this line as far as the villages of Bicker, Wigtoft, Sutterton, Kirton and Fosdyke and so on to the Sea Bank, including Wingland.

District No. 2 to be the remainder of the South Holland area.

In the event of a dispute regarding the proper allocation of any farms the matter shall be referred to a local Sub-Committee consisting of one member of the N.F.U. and one member of the N.U.A.W. with an independent chairman. The decision of the sub-committee shall be final.

In the event of a dispute regarding the proper rates for any job the matter shall be referred to the County Sub-Committee whose decision shall be final. No stoppage of work shall occur pending the settlement of a dispute, but the matter shall be referred at once to the respective Unions for prompt action.

The rates agreed upon represent an approximate increase of 10% upon last year's rates and it is hoped that this will give satisfaction to all concerned.

In view of the serious shipping position and especially in view of the country's military commitments during 1943 and the importance of agricultural production in this connection, the Holland War Agricultural Executive Committee, the National Farmers Union and the National Union of Agricultural Workers confidently call upon all farmers and workers loyally to honour the agreement reached and to do all in their power to harvest every ounce of foodstuffs.

(Signed on behalf of the Holland W.A.E.C.—ALEX WEST,
do.   do.   F.U.   —R. T. PROCTOR,
do.   do.   N.U.A.W.—A. E. MONKS.

DISTRICT NO. 1.

BEET. For acreages drilled with 18 inch coulters.
Chopping out (gapping)	28/- per acre.	2/- per acre up or down.
Singling	37/- per acre.	1/- per acre up or down.
Last hoeing and cleaning	35/- per acre.	2/- per acre up or down.
For all three operations	100/- per acre.	5/- per acre up or down.

For acreages drilled with 22½ inch coulters.
Chopping out (Gapping)	22/6 per acre.	2/- per acre up or down.
Singling	29/6 per acre.	1/- per acre up or down.
Last hoeing and cleaning	28/- per acre.	2/- per acre up or down.
For all three operations	80/- per acre.	5/- per acre up or down.

Proportionate rates for intermediate coulters

SEEDS
Mustard seed cutting (White)	88/- per acre.	20/- up 10/- down.
Beet and Mangel cutting	99/- per acre.	20/- up 10/- down.
Turnip and Swede cutting	90/- per acre.	10/- up or down.
Mustard seed cutting (Brown)	80/- per acre.	5/- up or down.
Mustard seed leading (White)	5/- per acre.	6d. up or down.
Mustard when threshed off field	6/- per acre.	6d. up or down.
Other seed leading	5/- per acre.	6d. up or down.

PEAS
Pea Cutting (Harvested)	49/6 per acre.	10/- up only
Pea Carting—		
(with 1 extra picker and elevator)	4/5 per acre.	6d. up or down.
(with only 1 picker, no elevator)	5/6 per acre.	6d. up or down.

CORN
Tying and stooking	33/- per acre.	2/6 up or down.
Mowing round	2/3 per acre.	3d. up or down.
Stooking after binder	7/2 per acre.	6d. up or down.
Carting (to include 1st rakings if tied)	4/5 per acre.	6d. up or down.
do. (to include both rakings)	4/8 per acre.	6d. up or down.
THATCHING (per running yard)	2/6 per acre.	3d. up or down.

POTATOES
Picking and into carts	115/6 per acre.	5/- up or down.

Graving and Strawing 1-7th of the picking price

BEET
Beet lifting into rows	100/- per acre.	5/- up or down.
Beet lifting into heaps	120/-	

Filling from rows 35s. per acre and filling from heaps 28s.

186

HOLLAND COUNTY COUNCIL

AIR RAID PRECAUTIONS

AIR RAID SHELTERS.

OWNERS of VAULTED BASEMENTS in THE BOROUGH OF BOSTON are urgently requested to Communicate AT ONCE with the Borough Engineer and Surveyor, Municipal Buildings, Boston.

H. C. MARRIS,

September 6th, 1939.

A.R.P. Controller.

SHOP BEFORE DUSK

The Stallholders of Boston Market appeal to the Public to attend Boston Market between the hours of 9 a.m. and 6 p.m., as the local authorities compel stallholders to be off the market by this time.

Morning shopping will be appreciated.

HELP YOURSELVES BY HELPING US

WINGS FOR VICTORY WEEK

GET READY for WINGS FOR VICTORY WEEK

MAY 22nd to 29th

and LEND every pound - you can possibly spare.

18 "BOSTON" BOMBERS FOR BOSTON

OUR AIM: £360,000

BOSTON & RURAL DISTRICT
1943
May 22nd to May 29th
Our Objective: 18 "BOSTON" BOMBERS
Our Aim £360,000

Via Singapore

We've got the blinkin' Zoo here,
    But we ain't in Regent's Park;
They never sweep the roads here,
    And the jungle's pretty dark;
We've muck up to our eyes here,
    And the towns ain't on the map,
A stick can be a snake here,
    And a tree may be a Jap.

It's hard tack and compo-rations,
    Dirty bilge and bully beef;
There's no time for steak and onions,
    When a Jap's behind a leaf.
But by heck! through swamp and mangrove
    We shall settle this old score;
We'll be coming back to England —
    And that's via Singapore.

SALUTE THE SOLDIER

Salute him with Savings. Ask yourself this: "Am I saving to the utmost limit to back up such men as these? Can I save more... to SALUTE THE SOLDIER."

Issued by the National Savings Committee

FOSTER BROTHERS GIFTS FOR DAD — AND THE LADS!

FAMOUS BROTHERS FAMOUS OVERCOATS
IN FOUR STYLES ONE PRICE

There are at least four of to-day's latest styles to choose from—including the popular full belted-style illustrated. Cloths include Tweeds also plain and check patterns in Air Force or Standard Blue & shades of green, fawn, brown & grey. **37/11**
Also 43/6 55/-

YOUTHS' SIZES Same style as men's. Smartly cut. *from* **32/6**
Other qualities 37/11 upwards.

FOR THE BOYS Grand selection of very hard wearing cloths. Full belted. For ages 7–14. **16/11**

KIDDIES' COATS Bring the youngster to Foster Brothers. Numerous styles at most reasonable prices.

Just Arrived! Toddlers Velour Legginette Sets. In nice pastel shades. **24/11**

GIFTS for the LADS
HOME OR ABROAD

SLIPOVERS Plain self colours or smart fancy patterns . . . **4/6**

CARDIGANS Warm and serviceable. Self colours or fancy designs. **7/6**

GLOVES Fleece, lambswool, or fur-lined. Wide choice. *from* **5/8**

FOSTER BROTHERS SMART LOUNGE SUITS
Single or Double Breasted styles. Latest cut in Fancy Worsted & Saxony effects. New shades of Air Force Blue. Also greys, browns, fawns. **37/11**
Also 43/6, 55/-

YOUTHS' SIZES In double breasted style. Very smartly cut. Newest patterns & cloths. *from* **29/6**

BOYS' 2-PIECE SPORTS SUITS Double seated knickers. Newest sporty patterns and shades. Fit boys ages 7–14. *from* **14/11**

The Bright Spot in the Blackout

TUNIC SHIRTS Smart new patterns with 2 cols. to match **5/6**

PULLOVERS 'V' neck or roll collar. Plain or fancy. **5/6**

SCARVES White silk scarves or smart fancy mixtures **2/11**

SOCKS Colours and patterns to tone with men's suit **1/9**

HATS The 'Front' 4/6 / The 'Postman' 7/11
CAPS Tweed Patterns 2/6 / Super Patterns 3/6
TIES The 'Prince' 1/- / The 'Bestall' (non-crease) 2/- / The 'West End' (Art Silk) 3/6

MEN'S GABARDINE RAINCOATS Self lined or check and half plush. Reliable and rainproof. *from* **25/- to 50/-**

Boys' School Regulation Blue Gabardine Raincoats. Oilskin interlined. *from* **17/6**

FOSTER BROTHERS
55/56, Market Place, BOSTON

"A British Family Firm, Established and Directed by FOSTERS since 1876"

The more GAS made the more war supplies are available

THE GAS INDUSTRY is a war industry. Every gas works is a war factory. Every ton of coal turned into gas means a greater supply of explosives, motor fuel, fertilizers, coke, tar, antiseptics and other materials essential to our war effort.

FROM EVERY HUNDRED TONS OF COAL used at the gas works we get, as well as gas and coke, 300 lbs. of explosive, 250 gallons of benzole, 2,500 lbs. of fertilizer. Our gas industry is twice the size of Germany's — an enormous wartime advantage to Britain provided that full use is made of it.

HOW GAS HELPS BRITAIN AT WAR

'Without the direct aid of the Gas Industry,' said the Director of Explosives in 1917, 'it would have been perfectly impossible for this country to have waged the campaigns of the last three years.'

The Minister of Supply, on a visit to a gasworks on February 16th, 1940, spoke of the way in which 'every ounce, every gramme of value is being extracted from coal, and turned to good use in the nation's interests.'

Every therm of GAS produced helps to win the war

Issued by

The Boston Gas Light & Coke Co.,

15, MARKET PLACE, BOSTON.

Works: Fydell St., Boston.   Tel. 2784.

Yes, it's NEW! Yes, it's BIG-SCALE!

a lively 12-horse engine — *easy-chair comfort for 5 people* — *ample luggage room*

YES! IT'S THE BRILLIANTLY STYLED
new AUSTIN '12'

Big in size, in performance, in comfort—a new, more generous Austin Twelve, full of interesting features for the owner-driver.

First, the size—biggest yet for a twelve. Many new comfort features such as optional air-conditioning and radio. Then, the redesigned engine—42 h.p. peak output —plenty of power and acceleration to spare under full family load. And—an entirely new feature—torsion-bar controlled suspension giving you a new experience in road-holding and cornering stability.

Remember, you buy a car but you invest in an Austin.

A TECHNICAL 2-MINUTES

42 h.p. engine (R.A.C. rating 12 h.p.). Increased power from high-compression aluminium cylinder-head and alloy pistons. New method of drawing oil from sump prevents impurities reaching engine. Mechanical petrol pump. Down-draught carburetter with air-silencer and oil-wetted cleaner. Radiator thermostat. Improved flexible mountings for engine and gearbox. Accessible gearbox dipstick. Improved clutch with lighter pedal action. Accessible 12-volt battery. Strong crossbraced chassis gives great rigidity. Long flat springs of low periodicity, lubricated directly by means of grooved leaves. Torsion-bar anti-roll control gives great stability. Full Girling brakes. Flexible-spoke steering wheel. Built-in radio and air-conditioning optional at extra charge. Draught excluders on pedals. Variable-strength instrument lights. In short a very fine car.

PLENTY OF ROOM IN THE BACK

The width across the arm-rests in this luxurious interior is no less than 59 inches. Three adults can sit back in comfort. Foot-rests, recessed into the back of the front seats, allow ample leg-room. Doorways are wide, head-room is generous. Side windows are fitted with louvres so that they may remain open when it rains.

Fixed-Head Saloon **£225** Sliding-Head Saloon **£235**
(at works)

Read the "Austin Magazine". 4d. every month.

INVEST IN AN AUSTIN — THE CAREFREE CAR

For the Best Selection of **GIFTS** Come to the

BOSTON Co-Operative Society

EVERYTHING for the Whole Family.
Toys for the Kiddies in Abundance.

We Still Give You Dividend —— We Still Give You Dividend

West Street - - - Boston.

Please Place Your Christmas Meat and Grocery Orders Early

WINTER ILLS
THE BEST REMEDY
'CLARKES BLOOD MIXTURE'

RHEUMATISM, LUMBAGO, NEURITIS
SCIATICA, RHEUMATIC JOINTS
SKIN COMPLAINTS, ECZEMA
ULCERS, SORES, RASHES, BOILS, etc.

THE DANGERS OF IMPURE BLOOD

Blood impurities poison the whole system, lower vitality and weaken the powers of resistance.

"Clarkes Blood Mixture" is the common-sense remedy; by cleansing the blood it gets to the root of your complaint and restores you to health. It is the original and genuine blood purifying medicine and is unequalled in the treatment of blood and skin complaints. Insist on "CLARKES BLOOD MIXTURE."

Sold everywhere
LIQUID
1/9, 3/-, & 5/-
also 12/- (three
times the 5/- size)

"CLARKES" BRAND
BLOOD PURIFYING MEDICINE
BLOOD MIXTURE
REGD. TRADE MARK

Sold everywhere
TABLETS
1/9, 3/- & 5/-
(5/- twice the
3/- size)

Have you tried CLARKES PILLS?
Brand
THE BEST LAXATIVE FOR GENERAL USE.

Clarkes Pills are purely vegetable and non-griping; unequalled in all cases of Constipation, Sluggish Liver, Biliousness. From all Chemists and Stores, price 1/3 and 3/-.

When the full history of the war is finally written

there will be much to enthral and fascinate besides the valorous deeds and enduring sacrifices of our fighting services.

There are the war workers whose skill and tempo produced the weapons that helped save us.

The Home Guard and all the other Civil Defence Services on whom fell the care of our homes and families.

The transport services, so efficiently controlled by the Ministry of War Transport—carrying unending supplies for home and abroad.

Finally, that great organisation known as The Ministry of Food, which has put through perhaps the biggest job of all. What a story remains to be told!

Brooke Bond Dividend Tea
1'7d - $\frac{1}{2}$-lb.

YOUR SOAP RATION
will go twice as far with
MAZO
soap energizing tablets

Almost too good to be true in these days of economy isn't it? But it *is* true; the quantity of soap you used, to need on washday will now do two Monday washes if you add Mazo to the water.

THINK WHAT THIS MEANS TO YOU

Twice the quantity of washing can now be done in the same time without any additional effort or extra soap.

'Compare the test tubes, containing the same amount of soap, and see how MAZO in test tube No. 1 increases the quantity of lather — proof positive that MAZO doubles the lather and cleansing energy of soap.

Not only will your soap ration go twice as far, but also, you will find washday much easier because the energized soap-suds do the hard work for you. Your washing is more thorough, yet quicker because the 'pep' that Mazo puts into soap-suds makes them work twice as hard, twice as fast and twice as efficiently.

There is nothing simpler to use than Mazo; just crumble the Mazo tablets into the water before the soap is added. You'll be amazed at the masses of richly energized suds you get, and at their extra cleansing power too, and these suds are gentle to even delicate garments.

It doesn't matter what you're washing, the golden rule is — if it's safe in soap and water, it's safe with Mazo added. Make sure you order Mazo today.

3 PACKETS FOR 1 COUPON

Add MAZO to get extra cleansing energy from soap
3d PER PACKET OF 5 TABLETS

RAIL TRANSPORT
is "Half the Battle"
WAGONS
loaded with
WAR FREIGHTS
run
10 MILLION
MILES
every day
BRITISH RAILWAYS
GWR · LMS LNER · SR
CARRY THE WAR LOAD

PARITY POOLS LTD.
67 TAVERNERS ROAD, PETERBOROUGH.

TEN MATCH 2ᴅ POINTS POOL 2 DIVS. 65% & 35%

S'hampton	Charlton	1
W. Ham	Tot'nham	2
Barnsley	Hud'sfield	3
Bury	Burnley	4
Derby	Notts. C.	5
D'caster	Sheff. W.	6
Everton	Man. U.	7
L'cester	Birm'ham	8
Man. C.	Bl'kpool	9
Wrexham	Liverp'l	10

CREDIT ONLY
Minimum Investment on this Coupon **1/-**
New Clients maximum credit 5/- after 4 weeks 10/- per week.

Sept. 18th
COUPONS MUST REACH US BY 2 p.m SATURDAY

2ᵈ 2ᵈ 2ᵈ 2ᵈ 2ᵈ 12 attempts 2/-

POOL 1	POOL 2	POOL 3	SAUCY SIX
9	3	4	ONE STAKE 6D.
RESULTS	DRAWS	AWAYS	ONE DIVIDEND

Airdrie	Clyde
S. Mirren	Hearts
S'hampton	Charlton
W. Ham	Tot'ham
Barnsley	Hud'sfield
Bury	Burnley
Arsenal	Portsm'th
Brentf'd	Chelsea
Brighton	Clapt'n O.
C. Palace	Reading
Fulham	Millwall
Luton	Aldershot
Q.P.R.	Watford
Aston V.	Wolves
Blackb'n	Bolton
Bradf'd C.	Leeds
Chester	Oldham
Chest'f'ld	Grimsby
Darl'ton	Mid'sbro
Derby	Notts. C.
D'caster	Sheff. W.
Everton	Man. U.
L'cester	Birm'ham
Man. C.	Bl'kpool
Mansf'ld	Roth'ham
N'wcastle	Bradford
N'thants	W. Brom.
Notts. F.	Lincoln
Sheff. U.	Halifax
S'thport	Rochdale
Stoke	Crewe
Sund'l'nd	Hart'p'ls
Tr'nmere	Stockp't
Walsall	Coventry
Wrexham	Liverp'l
York	Gatesh'd

6ᵈ 6ᵈ 6ᵈ 6ᵈ 6ᵈ 6ᵈ

Certified Divs. for Sept. 4th.
10 Match Points Pool—
1st—16 Points £71/5/6 to 2d
2nd—15 Points £5/1/8 to 2d
Saucy Six— £5/2/6 to 6d.
Pool 1— 40/- to 1/-
Pool 2— 60/- to 1/-
Pool 3— 720/- to 1/-

I enclose P.O. value
£   s.   d.
for previous investment dated
....

Members of H.M. Forces will appreciate that in the interests of National Security coupons can only be accepted from Home Addresses.

MINIMUM STAKE PER COLUMN 6D.

I agree to abide by your rules and conditions and will remit s.   d. next week, total staked on this coupon.

NAME IN BLOCK LETTERS:

ADDRESS ....

Claims
We pay winners on Mondays. Clients claiming must do so by Thursday following matches.

WORTH WHILE AGENCIES OPEN EVERYWHERE

★ BUTLIN'S
HOLIDAY CAMP
SKEGNESS
OPEN FOR INSPECTION
Sunday, August 20th.

2.30
Parade of BATHING BELLES
JUDGES :
ELIZABETH ALLAN
R. H. NAYLOR,
The Famous Astrologer
BILLY THORBURN,
The Radio Band Leader.
HUGHIE GREEN, STANFORD & McNAUGHTON,
The Radio and Stage Stars.

IN THE STADIUM
THE RACING CHEETAHS
The Fastest Animals in the World, the most modern of modern sports and full programme

ORGAN RECITALS : FAMOUS BANDS, etc.

ADMISSION TO THE CAMP 1/- (Children accompanied by Adults FREE—Car Park FREE) includes inspection of Main Buildings and Grounds, Use of Bathing Pool, Tennis Courts, Boating Lake, etc., the **SPECIAL EVENTS OF THE DAY** and Free Access to the Stadium.

'Phone 2961

ODEON REGD.

'Phone 2961

SOUTH SQUARE, BOSTON.

MONDAY, SEPTEMBER 4th. SIX DAYS.
CONTINUOUS FROM 5.45. MATINEES 2.15. TUESDAY AND FRIDAY EXCEPTED.

No Passion Greater
THAN THE VIOLENCE OF THWARTED LOVE!

Samuel Goldwyn, Hollywood's master showman, presents Emily Brontë's powerful conflict of emotions... an immortal screen version of an immortal novel!

I am Heathcliff... I married a woman I loathe... to spite the one woman I love!

SAMUEL GOLDWYN presents

WUTHERING HEIGHTS

The Strangest Love Story Ever Told

co-starring MERLE OBERON · LAURENCE OLIVIER · DAVID NIVEN

with Flora Robson · Donald Crisp
Geraldine Fitzgerald · *Screenplay by*
Ben Hecht and Charles MacArthur
Released thru United Artists
Directed by WILLIAM WYLER

SCREENING 2.50, 6.20, 8.45. (A)

ALSO

MUSICAL.   SPORT FILM.   NEWS REEL.

LAST PERFORMANCE COMMENCES 8.10.

The REGAL
SIGN OF LUXURY ENTERTAINMENT

Continuous from 6 p.m. Saturday from 2 p.m. Tel. 2921.
Matinees Monday and Wednesday at 2.15 p.m.

ALL THE WEEK

SHIRLEY TEMPLE
in
THE LITTLE PRINCESS

(Her First All Colour Film)
with RICHARD GREENE.
Screening at 3.13, 6.58 & 9.23

NEW THEATRE, BOSTON.
Monday, Sept. 4th, and during the week. Cont. from 6.15. Mat. Thurs. & Sat. at 2.15. Tel. 2135.

MON., TUES & WED.	THURS., FRI. & SAT.
TOD SLAUGHTER in THE FACE AT THE WINDOW SCREENING AT 7.27 & 9.42. ALSO PAUL KELLY In FORGED PASSPORT.	MELVYN DOUGLAS FAY WRAY in THE VAMPIRE BAT. SCREENING AT 7.28 & 9.43. With LIONEL ATWILL. Children under 16 not admitted.

SCALA, BOSTON.
Monday, Sept. 4th, and during the week. Cont. from 6.15. Mat. Wed. & Sat. at 2.15. 'Phone 2135.

Mon., Tues. & Wed.,	Thurs., Fri. & Sat.,
JOEL McCREA & ANDREA LEEDS in YOUTH TAKES A FLING. SCREENING AT 7.18 & 9.33. Also Glenda Farrell in EXPOSED.	DAVE WILLIS & PAT KIRKWOOD in ME AND MY PAL. SCREENING AT 7.14 & 9.29. Also THE JONES FAMILY in EVERYBODY'S BABY.

ODEON

Continuous DAILY from 2.0 p.m. 'Phone 2901

Thursday, May 10th—3 days

GREER GARSON — PIDGEON
Mrs. Parkington
EDWARD ARNOLD CLADYS COOPER
TOM DRAKE AGNES MOOREHEAD
2.35   5.20   8.5
CARIBBEAN ROMANCE
Musical Technicolor (U)

Monday, May 14th—3 days

ANNE BAXTER and JOHN HODIAK in
SUNDAY DINNER FOR A SOLDIER
2.15   5.35   8.55   (U)

MERLE OBERON and MIRIAM HOPKINS in
THESE THREE
(A)

SUNDAY, MAY 13th—JIMMY DURANTE and JANE WYMAN in
YOU'RE IN THE ARMY NOW (U)
LLOYD NOLAN in THE MAN WHO WOULDN'T DIE (A)

REGAL BOSTON

Phone 2921

Cont! from 5.30. Mats. Mon., Wed., Thurs. at 2.15. Sat. Cont. from 2.15

Thurs., Fri., Sat.—
6.18 and 8.40

LENI LYNN
WILL FYFFE
JACKIE HUNTER
in
GIVE ME THE STARS
Full Supporting Programme
Last Complete Perf. 7.48

Monday—For Six Days—
6.08 and 8.32

RITA HAYWORTH
in
COVER GIRL
Full Supporting Programme
Last Complete Perf. 7.44

SUNDAY, MAY 13th—
LEO GORCEY and
BOBBY JORDON in
KID DYNAMITE

One Performance at 6.45
ROBERTSON HARE
in
WOMEN AIN'T ANGELS

★ REGAL ★ REGAL ★ REGAL ★ REGAL ★

NEW THEATRE BOSTON

Cont. from 5.30
Mats.: Wed and Thurs. at 2.15
Sats.: Cont. from 2.15
'Phone 2135.

Thurs., Fri., Sat.—
6.48 and 9.24

MARGOT GRAHAME
PAUL CAVANAGH
in
CRIME OVER LONDON
Also STAN LAUREL and OLIVER HARDY in
FRATERNALLY YOURS
Last Complete Perf. 8.06

Mon. Tues. Wed.—
5.54 and 7.48

VERA LYNN
DONALD STEWART
in
ONE EXCITING NIGHT
Full Supporting Programme
Last Complete Perf. 7.24

More Individuality

THE MOOSE

The Americans always do things in a big way. Give them an inch and they'll make it an ell. Show them an Elk—and they'll turn it into a Moose, the largest Deer in the world.

Well, if you are going in for anything as magnificent as a deer you may as well make it a BIG deer. And if your aim is big business your printing must be impressive. You don't catch Moose in a mousetrap!

Not that deer-catching printing need in itself be dear. Oh dear, no! Let's show you!

GUARDIAN PRESS,
WEST STREET, - BOSTON

'Phone: 2266.

Guardian Press can now be found at Nelson Way, Boston. Tel: 01205 363497

LIST OF ABBREVIATIONS

(Not necessarily used in the book)

ACM	Air Chief Marshall - RAF
ARP	Air Raid Precautions
ARW	Air Raid Warden
ASR	Air Sea Rescue
AVM	Air Vice Marshall - RAF
B & G	Boat and Gun - local pub
BEM	British Empire Medal
'Bod'	Short for a person - 'Bods' persons
BRO	British Resistance Organisation
Civies	Civilian clothes
CWAEC	County War Agricultural Executive Committee
DCM	Distinguished Conduct Medal
DFM	Distinguished Flying Medal
Erk	A new recruit to any service
ENSA	Entertainment's National Services Association
Flt. Lt.	Flight Lieutenant - RAF
FU	Farmer's Union
GD	General Duties - RAF
GG	Ground Gunner - Prior to forming RAF Regiment
GI	Government Issue - American
GHQ	General Headquarters
GPO	General Post Office
Gy	Grimsby
HG	Home Guard

HSL	High Speed Launch
HQ	Headquarters
HM	Her (or His) Majesty
ITMA	'It's That Man Again' - Radio programme
Lt.	Lieutenant
LARG	Lincolnshire Aviation Recovery Group
LHS	Left-hand side
LDV	Local Defence Volunteer
	Nicknamed - 'LOOK, DUCK AND VANISH'
LST	Landing Ship Tanks
LNER	London North Eastern Railway
MC	Military Cross
Mk.	Mark
MoD	Ministry of Defence
MCU	Motor Craft Unit
NAAFI	Navy, Army, Air Force Institute
NCO	Non-Commissioned Officer
NUAW	National Union Agricultural Workers
OP	Operational Post
oz.	Ounces
PC	Policeman
PM	Prime Minister
PoW	Prisoner of War
PO	Pilot Officer
RAF	Royal Air Force
RAFA	Royal Air Forces Association
RBL	Royal British Legion

RHS	Right-Hand Side
RML	Rescue Motor Launch
RNLI	Royal National Lifeboat Institution
ROC	Royal Observer Corps
Sgt.	Sergeant
SNCO	Senior Non-Commissioned Officer
SOP	Sleeping Out Pass
Sqd. Ldr.	Squadron Leader - RAF
UK	United Kingdom
USA	United States of America
USAF	United States Air Force
USAAF	United States Army Air Force
VC	Victoria Cross
VE	Victory in Europe
VJ	Victory over Japan
WAAF	Women's Auxiliary Air Force later Women's Royal Air Force
WAAC	Women's Army Auxiliary Corps
Wg. Cdr.	Wing Commander - RAF
WI	Women's Institute
WRNS	Women's Royal Naval Service
WLA	Women's Land Army
WTC	Women's Timber Corps
W/T	Wireless Transmitter
WO	Warrant Officer
WVS	Women's Voluntary Service
£.s.d.	Old currency UK pound, shillings and pennies sign
£.p.	New currency UK pound and pence sign

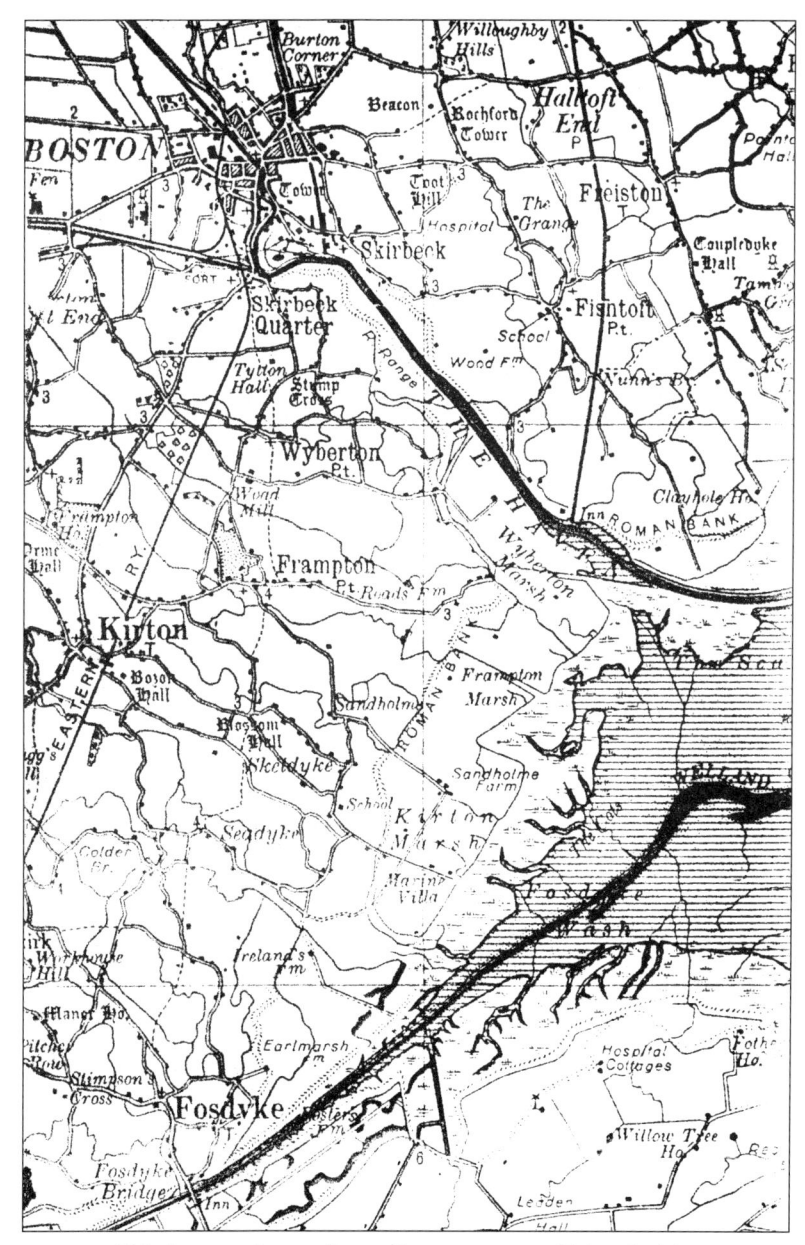

This is part of one of two German maps of Lincolnshire
I acquired when in France in 1944.

Stanley Naylor, 2000

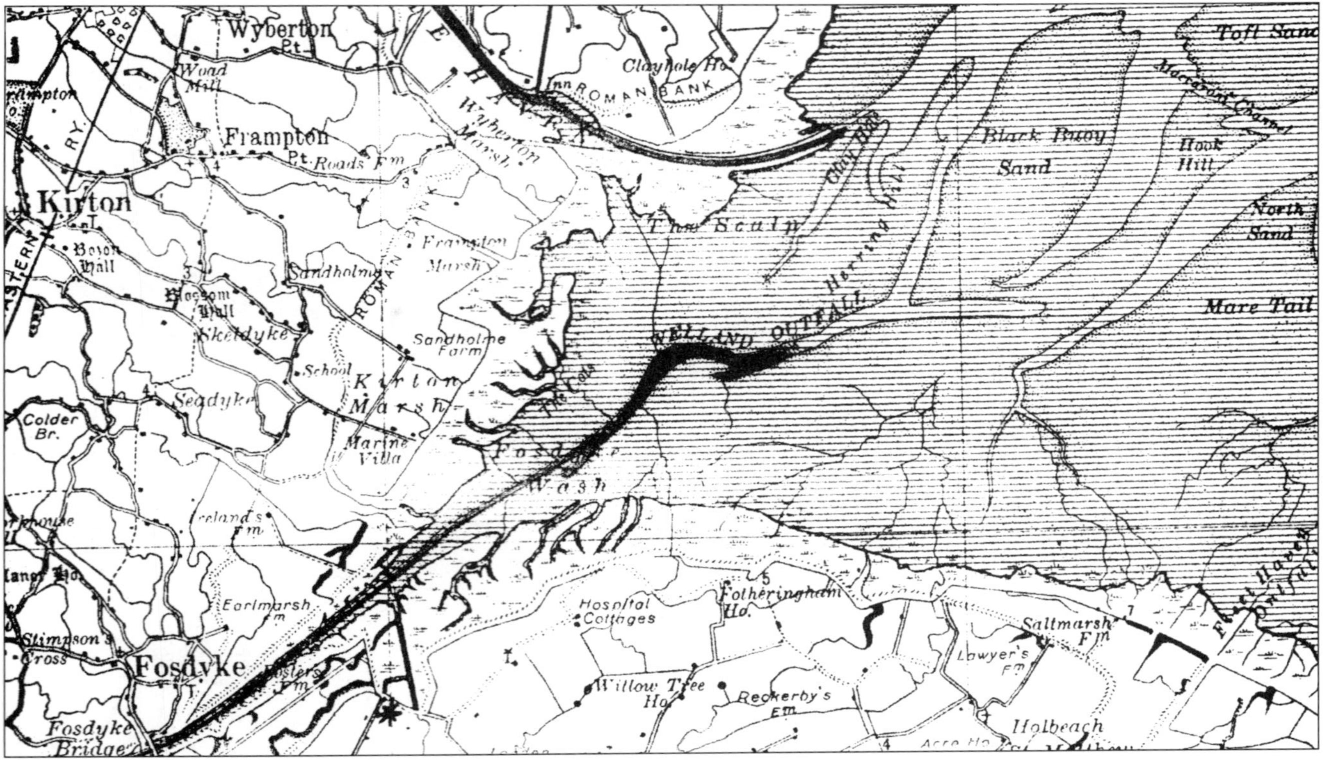

This is part of one of two German maps of Lincolnshire I acquired when in France in 1944.

Stanley Naylor, 2000

RECOMMENDED BOOKS

Rauceby Reflections by Mrs Gwyneth Stratten.

This is the history of No. 4 RAF Hospital, Rauceby that was operational from 1940 to 1947 and had many famous names as patients including: ACM Sir Augustus Walker; WC Guy Gibson VC and Fl. Sgt. John Hannah who won his VC at the age of eighteen in 1940.

Priced at £2.50 plus 50p postage and packing. Make cheques payable to Rauceby Hospital and post to: Rauceby Hospital, Grantham Road, South Rauceby, Sleaford, Lincolnshire, NG34 8PR, UK.

Aviation Unearthed compiled by David Stubley.

Stories behind aircraft recovery written by members of the British Aviation Archaelogical Council.

Price £4.95 plus 50p postage and packing. Make cheques payable to BAAC and post to: David Stubley, 33 Grosvenor Road, Frampton, Boston, Lincolnshire, PE20 1DB, UK.

Civilians At War edited by James P. Allen.

The Second World War 1939 - 1945 Remembered. Horrendous war stories told vividly by the people who lived them, with unbelievable pictures of destruction. A souvenir book well worth the modest cost of £3.00 inclusive of postage and packing. Make cheques/postal orders payable to Change Charity and post to: James P. Allen, Change Charity, c/o The Markwick Centre, Dampier Street, Yeovil, Somerset, BA21 4EN.

Silksheen by Geoff D. Copeman a Midland Counties Publication.

The history of East Kirkby airfield from the days of the 'decoy' airfield, through the war years when the 'drome was occupied by the RAF. Then through the post war years when the USAF were residents and on to the present day museum.

Available from Midland Counties Publications and Lincolnshire Aviation Heritage Centre, East Kirkby, Spilsby, Lincolnshire, PE23 4DE.

The Isle of Dogs, A Brief History, Volume 1 - 1066/1918.

120 A4 pages, an illustrated history up to the end of World War I. Available from the Isle of Dogs Trust for £12.00 including postage. Make cheques/postal orders payable to Island History Trust and post to: Dockland Settlement, 197 East Ferry Road, London, E14 3BA.

WI 'Live and Learn', story of Denham College 1948 to 1969 by Barbara Kaye.

WI 'Village Voices', A Portrait of Change in England's Green and Pleasant Land 1915 to 1990 by Piers Dudgeon.

'The Last Ditch' by Davis Lampe published by Cassell of London 1968. A very detailed account of the undercover British Resistance Organisation.

LINCOLNSHIRE COUNTRY LIFE BESIDE THE WASH 1920's to 1939

(Another book by Stanley Naylor)

There are two stories, the first is based on Kirton Skeldyke in the Fens nestling beside the Wash estuary. This was a typical farming community and could be in any Fenland area in the country, although the inhabitants of Skeldyke were true 'Yellowbellies'.

Work on the farm was hard for man and horse. There were no mod cons, no electricity meant no television or computers. No running water meant no dishwashers, washing machines or en-suite facilities, the privy was down the garden path and bathing was done in a tin tub. Business people mainly owned cars and telephones. The carriers cart with two horses passed through the hamlet Wednesdays and Saturdays on its way to Boston markets, this was prior to buses.

The school was demolished in April 2000 and the church, chapel and pub are all residential. The 'Nook' a 'mud and stud' house is still occupied today, but the thatched roof has been replaced with tiles.

Dame Sara Ann Swift, born in Skeldyke 1854, founded the Royal College of Nursing. Sir Peter Scott, painter, writer and ornithologist of distinction, visited Kirton Marsh.

The second story involves Kirton marsh that is in the NW corner of the Wash at the mouth of the River Welland. The Wash is one of two of the largest estuarine flats in Great Britain and has international recognition for its contribution to the support of world populations of many wildfowl and wading bird species.

There are over ninety photographs, nine pages of adverts, 3 pages of village news from 1934/36, with prices and wages that are astounding. There are nine pages of dialect used in Skeldyke prior to World War II, plus poems and recipes.

The price is £12.95 inclusive of post and packing (UK only, overseas add £1.50 for extra postage) from: Stanley Naylor, 15 Edinburgh Crescent, Kirton, Boston, Lincolnshire, PE20 1JT, United Kingdom.

MUSEUMS OF INTEREST AS VISITED BY THE AUTHOR

USAAF 388th COLLECTION
Hillside Farm, Market Western, Suffolk. IP22 2NX
Contact Curator David Sarson on 01359 221257
Open third Sunday in the month April to October 1.00pm to 5.00pm
Free admission - donations gratefully accepted

The collection consists of World War II memorabilia, uniforms, personal items, equipment, photographs and armament are meticulously displayed, housed in an original 388th Bomb Group Nessen Hut.

NORFOLK AND SUFFOLK AVIATION MUSEUM
(East Anglia's Aviation Heritage Centre)
The Street, Flixton, Nr Bungay, Suffolk. NR35 1NZ
Summer opening: Sundays to Thursdays - 10.00am to 5.00pm
Admission and car parking free - donations welcomed

Incorporating: Bomber Command Museum, Air Sea Rescue, Coastal Command Museum, Royal Observer Corps Museum and USAAF 446th Bomb Group Museum.

THE BRITISH RESISTANCE ORGANISATION MUSEUM
(Not yet visited by the author)
Parham Airfield, South of Framlingham, Suffolk, on the B1116

LINCOLNSHIRE AVIATION HERITAGE CENTRE
East Kirkby, near Spilsby, Lincolnshire. PE23 4DE
Telephone: 01790 763207
Open Monday - Friday 10.00am to 5.00pm
Saturday 11.00am to 5.00pm ~~Sunday 10.00am to 6.00pm~~
(Close dusk in winter months)
Admission charged

Walk back in time and re-live life on a wartime bomber airfield! Experience the sights and sounds of a Lancaster bomber taxiing down the runway. Visit a renovated control tower representative of a typical World War II 'ops' night. See a Ford Jeep, Foam Tender and Crew Bus. David Brown Tug Tractor, Bedford 'Queen Mary' and a BSA Despatch Motorcycle. Have a cup of tea in the 'NAAFI' and view the huge display of photographs and memorabilia.

ALLIED FORCES MILITARY MUSEUM
Stickford, Boston, Lincolnshire
Telephone: 01205 480317
Open Monday to Friday 10.00am to 5.00pm
(A telephone call might be appropriate)
Admission free

An excellent display of American vehicles and memorabilia.

ALFORD MANOR HOUSE
Alford Civic Trust Ltd.
West Street, Alford, Lincolnshire. LN13 9DJ
Open Tuesdays, Fridays and Bank Holidays throughout the summer

Although this is a 'living' museum spanning 300 years, there are many things referring to the Second World War era.

MERLINS
Fairways, East Kirkby, Spilsby, Lincolnshire. PE23 4BY
Web site: www.merlins.flyer.co.uk
Open Tuesdays, Thursdays, Fridays and Saturdays 10.00am to 4.00pm

Merlins have a good selection of RAF and USAAF equipment, paperwork, clothing, aviation and military books.

LILLIAN REAM PHOTOGRAPHIC COLLECTION
Many photographs are on display in albums at the
Tourist Information Centre, 2-3 Bridge Street, Wisbech

THE ISLE OF DOGS, LONDON
Dockland Settlement, 197 East Ferry Road, London. E14 3BA
Telephone: 020 7987 6041
Web site: www.islandhistory.org.uk

The Island History Trust is a small museum with a collection of 5,000 photographs all captioned and indexed by name and subject, covering the past 100 years. The Trust publishes a newsletter and an annual calendar as well as various books. (See book section for latest publication). The Trust Museum can be visited any Tuesday or Wednesday afternoons and the first Sunday of each month, from 1.30pm to 4.30pm.

THORPE CAMP VISITOR CENTRE
Ex RAF Woodhall Spa, Tattershall Thorpe, Coningsby, Lincolnshire.
Telephone: 01526 342249
Web site: www.thorpecamp.org.uk
Open Easter to end of October Sundays/Bank Holidays
2.00pm to 5.00pm
Small entrance fee